Sunset
COOK BOOK OF
BREADS

BY THE EDITORS OF SUNSET BOOKS
AND SUNSET MAGAZINE

LANE BOOKS · MENLO PARK, CALIFORNIA

Library of Congress Catalog Card Number 66-15331. Title Number 274

Second Edition. Copyright © 1966 by Lane Magazine & Book Company, Menlo Park, California

Third Printing July 1967

CONTENTS

YEAST BREADS

Some good cooks frankly admit that they have never baked a really successful loaf of yeast bread. If you're in this category, or if you have never even tried to make yeast bread, the basic information on these next few pages is addressed to you. Follow the ten steps in the recipe for Basic White Bread and we think you'll discover that there are satisfactions in bread making that can't be duplicated by any other cooking skill.

If, on the other hand, you have already mastered the techniques of bread baking, we suggest you skip this introductory information and go on to other recipes. You'll see some delightful ways to vary the shape and flavor of yeast bread when you bake it yourself. One kind is as easy as the other, once you've mastered the basic steps.

TEMPERATURE AND YEAST

Choose a time to start making bread when your kitchen is warm (about 80°). When you work with yeast, temperature is of special importance. A living organism, yeast does its work best at just the right warmth. When there's not enough heat, its action is sluggish; when there's too much, the yeast dies. If you've ever had bread dough that refused to rise, chances are that you inadvertently killed the yeast action.

If you have been unable to bake successful bread in the past, or if you are a novice at bread baking, use thermometers to check air and liquid temperature—an ordinary room thermometer and a candy

From one basic dough—the brioche recipe on page 27—come these many forms of delicious golden breads.

thermometer will do nicely. After a few baking successes, you can do without these aids. If you don't have a candy thermometer, test the temperature of the liquid by placing a few drops on your wrist. If you cannot feel it, or if it feels comfortably warm (not hot), the temperature is 98°, or just a few degrees above body temperature.

THE "WHYS" OF BREAD MAKING

To understand what goes on when you bake a loaf of bread, let's analyze a recipe to see what each ingredient does.

Flour contains a protein substance called gluten, which has the unique property when wet of stretching to become an elastic framework. The amount and strength of gluten varies with the flour. You'll notice that bread recipes seldom state an exact amount of flour. This is because the amount and quality of gluten are never exactly the same, and flour's absorptive properties vary with temperature and humidity. These are also the reasons why exact times for beating and kneading cannot be given— rather you must learn to recognize when the mixture "feels" right.

Recently a new instant-type all-purpose flour has been introduced by manufacturers. However, since many of the recipes in this book have not been tested with the new flour, we recommend that you use regular all-purpose flour for tested results and experiment with the instant-type flour when you are so inclined.

Milk or water are the liquids usually used for making yeast bread. Milk gives bread a velvety grain and adds nutrients. Breads made with all water have heavier, crisper crust—French bread is an example. Sometimes other liquids, such as fruit juices, are used for special flavors. Water is the best medium for dissolving dry yeast, so whatever recipe you use, be sure at least ¼ cup of the liquid is water to dissolve the yeast.

Yeast comes in both dry and compressed forms; they give equally good results, but the dry form is less perishable. (To determine whether compressed yeast is usable, crumble it between your fingers. If it crumbles easily, it is still good.) When the yeast is put into action in the dough, fermentation begins, and carbon dioxide is given off. This gas gets trapped in the glutenous framework of the dough and causes it to stretch and rise.

Fat is in bread mainly for flavor, but it also contributes to its tenderness. Salad oil is the most convenient fat to use because it is already a liquid. But many cooks prefer to use melted butter or margarine for the flavor. You may want also to brush hot loaves of bread lightly with butter to give them softer, shinier crusts.

Salt and sugar are for flavor, too. You can vary the flavor of bread by using brown sugar, molasses, honey, or syrup in place of granulated sugar; but if you use a liquid sugar, reduce the other liquid in the recipe by an equal amount. The more sugar in a recipe, the browner the crust becomes.

Eggs and other ingredients are sometimes added to bread for special flavors. In addition, eggs add richness, tenderness, and a golden color. When you use egg in our basic recipe, beat it slightly, then let its volume replace an equal amount of the liquid in the recipe. Additions such as spices, herbs, raisins, or nuts can be added to the bread recipe without adjusting proportions.

WHAT TO DO IF . . .

If there's no warm spot in your kitchen when it's time for the bread to rise, use a heavy pottery bowl; warm it with hot water before you start, and repeat this before placing the dough back in the bowl to rise. Set it to rise on a high shelf (heat rises). Or set the bowl of dough in the sink in warm water (around 80°); add warm water as it cools. Or let it rise in an *unheated* oven with a large pan of hot water on a shelf below.

If you are interrupted while making bread, there are several solutions, depending on what you're doing at the time. If you're beating or kneading it, don't worry about stopping; you will simply find the dough easier to handle when you return; if you're likely to be gone for more than 15 minutes, however, cover the bowl (or if the dough is on the board, invert the bowl over it) to prevent drying.

If it's not convenient to shape the loaves when the dough has doubled, punch it down to get out all the air, cover, and let rise again. Each subsequent rising period will take a little less time.

If the shaped dough in the pans rises too much (overproof) before you get it into the oven, turn it out, knead or squeeze out all the air bubbles, reshape, and let rise in the pans again.

HOW TO FREEZE UNBAKED BREAD DOUGH

You can freeze unbaked bread and roll dough for short periods. However, for best results, plan to keep them for no longer than two weeks in your freezer.

To freeze unbaked bread, shape the loaves, wrap them in plastic film or foil, and freeze, being careful that the dough is on a flat surface so it will keep its shape until frozen. When you shape the dough, be sure that it fits easily into the baking pan. It will spread a little before it freezes. When you are ready to finish the bread, remove a loaf from the freezer, put it in a greased loaf pan (the size specified in the recipe) and let it thaw and rise in a warm place until almost doubled in bulk—about 6 hours for a standard size loaf. (Or thaw the loaf in your refrigerator overnight. The next day, unwrap and put into a loaf pan, and let rise in a warm place—it will take about 2 hours.)

To freeze rolls, shape them on greased baking sheets or in muffin pans, as indicated in the recipe. Cover the pans of shaped rolls with plastic film or foil and set them directly into the freezer. As soon as they're completely frozen, remove rolls from baking pans and store them in freezer bags or other freezer wrappings. Exceptions are the rolls shaped in muffin pans, which are best frozen and stored in the pans. Carefully label each package. To use the frozen rolls, remove them from the freezer

Many breads and rolls can be shaped, wrapped, frozen, and stored for future family or company meals.

about 2 hours before you plan to bake them. Arrange them again on the greased baking pans about 1 inch apart. Cover pans loosely with a clean cloth and set in a warm place to thaw and rise until almost doubled in size (takes 1½ to 2 hours). Bake as directed in recipe.

If you should run short of time for shaping rolls, you can wrap and freeze the dough at the time you punch it down after the first rising. When you want to use it, the dough must be thawed (about 3 hours at room temperature or overnight in the refrigerator), then shaped, and allowed to rise.

BASIC WHITE BREAD

For this basic recipe, you'll need two bread pans (either 5¼ by 9¼-inch size, or 4½ by 8½); they can be metal or glass. For mixing, a heavy pottery bowl is ideal; it holds the heat best, but any bowl of about 4-quart size will do.

You'll need about 6 cups of flour, but sift an amount well in excess of this into a large bowl for convenience in dipping it out as you need it. Heat the milk to just below the boiling point to scald it, then let it cool to about 105° if you are using dry yeast; or cool to 95° if you are using compressed yeast. (An easier way is to use 1 cup evaporated milk, which needs no scalding, with 1 cup very hot water—the resulting temperature is usually about right. Or dissolve ¼ cup dry skim milk in 1⅞ cups (2 cups minus 2 tablespoons) warm water.

To make one loaf of bread from basic recipe, halve all ingredients except yeast and warm water; use 1 package yeast dissolved in ¼ cup warm water. In step 8, shape into one loaf.

¼ cup warm water (105° for dry
    yeast, 95° for compressed yeast)
1 package yeast, active dry or
    compressed
2 cups scalded milk (cool to 105°
    or 95°)
2 tablespoons melted butter or
    margarine, or salad oil
2 teaspoons salt
2 tablespoons granulated sugar
6 to 6½ cups regular all-purpose
    flour (sift before measuring)

STEP 1. Pour water into bowl; add yeast and stir until dissolved. Stir in the scalded and cooled milk, then add the melted butter, salt, and sugar; stir until well blended.

STEP 2. Stir in 3 cups of flour, 1 cup at a time. Add 4th cup of flour, and beat until dough is smooth and elastic (rest when you get tired). Mix the 5th cup of flour in to make a stiff dough.

STEP 3. Measure 6th cup of flour, sprinkle about half of it on board. Turn out dough onto heavily floured area of board. Keep a coating of flour on the dough as you begin to knead.

STEP 4. With floured hands, fold dough toward you with fingers; push firmly away with heel of your hand. Add more flour to board as it's kneaded in—until the dough no longer sticks.

STEP 5. Kneading is finished when non-sticky dough is smooth and satiny. Put dough in greased bowl, grease top lightly. Cover bowl and set in warm place (about 80°) to rise.

STEP 6. Let dough rise until almost doubled (about 1½ hours at 80°). Test by inserting two fingers about ½ inch into risen dough—if indentations remain, the dough is ready to shape.

STEP 7. Punch dough down; squeeze out air bubbles with your hands; shape into a smooth ball. Grasp in center of ball and squeeze dough to divide into equal portions for the 2 loaves.

STEP 8. Form each loaf by squeezing dough to press out air bubbles; shape into smooth oval. Turn over in one hand; with other hand, pinch seam in center, turn ends, seal as shown.

HERB BREADS

Follow Basic White Bread recipe. If you want to make two kinds, in Step 4 divide dough into two parts; knead each part separately, kneading a different herb into each. Select from these herbs, using the following amounts for each half of the dough: 1 tablespoon dill weed; 1 tablespoon savory; 1½ teaspoons basil; 1½ teaspoons oregano; 1½ teaspoons thyme; or 2¼ teaspoons marjoram. If you want to make 6 small loaves, in Step 7 through 10 divide each half of dough into three parts; shape as for large loaf. Let rise in 6 greased pans (3¼ by 5½ inches); bake (at 375°) about 25 minutes.

STEP 9. Put shaped loaves in greased pans, seams down. Cover; let rise in warm place until almost doubled (about 45 minutes). Put in 375° oven (350° if you use glass pans).

EGG BRAID

Follow Basic White Bread recipe with these changes: In Step 1, break 2 eggs into a 2-cup measure; beat in scalded and cooled milk to make 2 cups, and use this mixture in place of all milk. In Step 8, divide the dough for each loaf into 3 parts; roll each into a strand. Braid each trio of strands together, pinching ends to seal. In Step 9, let rise on lightly greased baking sheet. Brush with slightly beaten egg before baking. Bake (at 375°) for 30 to 35 minutes or until nicely browned.

TOMATO CARAWAY SNACK LOAF

Follow Basic White Bread recipe with these changes: In Step 1, use 2 cups warm tomato juice in place of milk; add 1 tablespoon caraway seed. In Steps 7 through 9, divide dough into 4 equal parts. Roll each into a long, thin loaf, about 14 inches long; let rise on lightly greased baking sheets. Brush with slightly beaten egg, and sprinkle each loaf with about 1 teaspoon caraway seed before baking. Bake (at 375°) for 25 to 30 minutes, or until lightly browned.

STEP 10. Bake until nicely browned and just starting to pull away from pan sides (about 45 minutes). Remove from oven; turn loaves out of pans to cool before slicing or wrapping.

Clockwise starting at upper left: Egg Braid, Orange-Raisin-Nut Bread, Tomato Caraway Snack Loaf, Onion Bread (round) and Diet Bread, French Bread, Herb Breads, Cinnamon Swirl Loaf.

POPPY SEED BUBBLE LOAF

Follow Basic White Bread recipe with these changes: In Steps 7 through 10, pinch off pieces of dough (after it's punched down) to make tiny balls about 1 inch in diameter. Melt 4 tablespoons butter. Measure ¼ cup poppy seed. Dip top of each ball first into butter, then into poppy seed, and pile all the balls in one lightly greased (10-inch) tube pan, seed side up; let rise. Bake (at 375°) about 55 minutes.

ORANGE-RAISIN-NUT BREAD

Follow Basic White Bread recipe, but in Step 1, use 2 cups warm orange juice instead of milk; add 1 tablespoon grated orange peel, 1 cup seedless raisins, and ½ cup chopped walnuts.

DIET BREAD

Follow Basic White Bread recipe with these changes: In Step 1, use all water, or ¼ cup powdered skim milk stirred into 1⅞ cups (2 tablespoons less than 2 cups) water, in place of milk. Omit the shortening, salt, and sugar.

ONION BREAD

Follow Basic White Bread recipe with these changes: In Step 1, use 1 can (10½ oz.) onion soup and enough warm water to make 2 cups liquid in place of all milk; omit sugar, use only 1 teaspoon salt, and add 1 tablespoon instant minced onion. In Steps 8 and 9, shape each loaf into a ball and place in a 1-quart round casserole; bake same as basic loaves.

CINNAMON SWIRL LOAF

Follow Basic White Bread recipe with these changes: In Steps 8 and 9 roll out dough for each loaf into a rectangle about 6 by 16 inches. Mix 4 tablespoons sugar with 4 tablespoons cinnamon; sprinkle half evenly over top of each rectangle. Beginning with a narrow side, roll each tightly into a loaf; seal ends and bottom by pinching together to make seam. Let rise in 2 baking pans (5¼ by 9¼-inch size).

FRENCH BREAD

Follow Basic White Bread recipe with these changes: In Step 1, use water in place of milk; omit shortening. In Steps 8 through 10, shape into two oblong loaves; let rise on a lightly greased baking sheet. Brush with water and make diagonal slashes in top with a sharp knife before baking. Place in a hot oven (400°)—with shallow pan of hot water in oven bottom—until crusty and brown, about 45 minutes.

TO MAKE DARK BREADS

By substituting other flours for the white flour in the Basic White Bread recipe that follows, you can duplicate almost all your favorite kinds of dark bread. A number of possible combinations are given below and opposite. Most supermarkets carry whole wheat, graham, cracked wheat, buckwheat, and rye flours. Health food stores usually carry an even wider selection.

When you use these variety flours, here are some points to keep in mind: As the ratio of dark flour to regular all-purpose flour increases, so also does the rising time of your bread (instead of 1½ hours, it may take 2 hours or more). Don't expect the darker breads to double in bulk when they rise; however, the same test described in Step 6 of the Basic White Bread recipe is your guide to judge when the bread has risen enough. Because the finished loaves of bread are smaller and more compact than white bread, you'll have more attractively shaped loaves if you use medium-sized bread pans (4½ by 8½ inches or 3¾ by 7½ inches) instead of the standard (5¼ inches).

Whole wheat is the only flour we suggest substituting for the entire amount of regular all-purpose flour. All other flours (including cracked wheat, graham, and rye) are best if not more than 3 cups are used—the other 3 cups in the recipe might be whole wheat or regular all-purpose flour. Such ingredients as whole bran, rye meal, wheat germ, and soy and buckwheat flours are best used in even smaller proportions.

When you substitute other flours in our Basic White Bread, follow this order for mixing the flours with the liquid ingredients: The first, second, and sixth (or last) cups of flour should be regular all-purpose or whole wheat. The other flours can be the third, fourth, and fifth cups you add.

LIGHT RYE BREAD

Follow Basic White Bread recipe, using 1 cup rye flour and 5 cups regular all-purpose. This has greater volume than the darker breads, and is best baked in standard 5¼ by 9¼-inch pans.

MEDIUM RYE BREAD

Follow Basic White Bread recipe, using 2 cups rye flour and 4 cups regular all-purpose flour.

SWEDISH ORANGE RYE BREAD

Follow Basic White Bread recipe, using 2 cups rye flour and 4 cups regular all-purpose flour as for Medium Rye Bread. In Step 1, add 2 tablespoons grated orange peel and 1 tablespoon caraway, anise, or fennel seed.

DARK RYE BREAD

Follow Basic White Bread recipe, using 3 cups rye and 3 cups regular all-purpose flour. In Step 1, omit sugar; instead of all milk, use ½ cup light or dark molasses with 1½ cups milk.

OATMEAL BREAD

Follow Basic White Bread recipe, using 4 cups of regular all-purpose flour and 2 cups oat flour (found in health food stores, or make it by whirling rolled oats in electric blender until fine).

PUMPERNICKEL BREAD

Follow Basic White Bread recipe. For flour use 1 cup whole bran cereal, 2 cups rye flour, and 3 cups whole wheat flour. In Step 1, add 1 tablespoon caraway seed.

100% WHOLE WHEAT BREAD

Follow Basic White Bread recipe, using all whole wheat flour. In Step 1, omit sugar; use ½ cup honey, molasses, or maple syrup with 1½ cups milk instead of all milk.

SOY-GRAHAM BREAD

Follow Basic White Bread recipe, using 1 cup soy flour, 2 cups graham, 3 cups regular all-purpose.

DARK MIXED GRAIN BREAD

Follow Basic White Bread recipe. For flour use ½ cup wheat germ, ½ cup buckwheat flour, 1 cup rye, and 4 cups whole wheat. Omit sugar; use ½ cup dark molasses with 1½ cups milk instead of all milk.

50% WHOLE WHEAT, GRAHAM, OR CRACKED WHEAT BREAD

Follow Basic White Bread recipe, using 3 cups of any of these flours, with 3 cups regular all-purpose. Use brown sugar instead of granulated sugar, if you wish.

FRUIT-NUT GRAHAM BREAD

Make 50% Graham Bread as described above. In Step 7, knead in 1 cup chopped mixed glacéed fruit or chopped pitted dates and 1 cup chopped nuts. After loaves are baked, glaze while still warm with ½ cup sifted powdered sugar mixed with 1 tablespoon water.

Combine Postum, hot water, molasses, bread crumbs. Add yeast-sugar-ginger mixture.

Before baking, brush loaf with mixture of water and Postum to give crust dark, deep color.

The baked bread resembles in flavor, color the black bread of Old Europe's peasantry.

PEASANT'S BLACK BREAD

If you like coarse, dark breads, you'll be interested in this version of European peasant bread. It has a rich, unsweet, parched grain flavor. Try it in sandwiches with ham or salami and cheese, or serve it already buttered with a meal or as accompaniment to a bowl of thick, hot soup.

When you make your first loaf of peasant bread, start by toasting plain fine, dry bread crumbs until they are parched but not burned. To make each successive loaf darker, save the end pieces and crusts of each loaf you bake and crush them into fine crumbs. Toast these crumbs again, and put them into the next batch of bread. You can store the toasted crumbs in a plastic bag in the freezer if you don't expect to bake another batch of bread immediately.

> *3 teaspoons Postum*
> *2 cups hot water*
> *4 tablespoons dark molasses*
> *2 cups fine bread crumbs,*
> *   toasted until very dark*
> *3 packages yeast, active dry or*
> *   compressed*
> *½ cup warm water (lukewarm*
> *   for compressed yeast)*
> *1 teaspoon sugar*
> *¼ teaspoon ground ginger*
> *3 cups rye flour*
> *¼ cup (⅛ lb.) melted butter*
> *   or shortening*
> *2 teaspoons salt*
> *2 cups unsifted regular*
> *   all-purpose flour*
> *1 teaspoon Postum mixed with*
> *   2 teaspoons water*

In a large bowl, dissolve the 3 teaspoons Postum in the 2 cups hot water. Stir in the molasses and bread crumbs. Let stand until mixture is cooled to lukewarm and crumbs are soaked and soft.

In a small bowl, dissolve the yeast in the ½ cup warm water, and stir in sugar and ginger. Let stand for 15 minutes. Stir this mixture into the lukewarm bread crumb mixture. Add the rye flour and stir until well combined, then stir in the melted butter and salt (mixture will seem dry). Spread the all-purpose flour on a bread board; turn the mixture out onto the flour. Invert the mixing bowl over the dough and let stand for about 15 minutes. Knead until a smooth stiff dough forms, about 10 minutes. Clean bowl out and grease lightly. Place kneaded dough in bowl, turn over to grease top of loaf, cover, and let rise in a warm place until doubled in bulk, about 1½ hours.

Turn out onto lightly floured board, knead lightly to remove air bubbles, and shape into a loaf about 15 inches long. Place on a well-greased cooky sheet, cover lightly, and let rise in a warm place for about 30 minutes. Just before baking, brush loaf with the mixture of Postum and water. Bake in a hot oven (400°) for 40 to 45 minutes, or until loaf is quite dry.

This bread will have a thick crust when freshly baked, but after it stands a day or two, the crust softens. Store in a plastic bag. Makes 1 large loaf.

ONION-HERB BATTER BREAD

If you bake this batter bread loaf to serve warm for a company meal, a wonderful onion and herb aroma of baking will greet your guests.

> ½ cup milk
> 1½ tablespoons sugar
> 1 teaspoon salt
> 2¼ teaspoons butter or margarine
> 1 package yeast, active dry or
>   compressed
> ½ cup warm water (lukewarm
>   for compressed yeast)
> 2¼ cups regular all-purpose flour
>   (sift before measuring)
> 1 tablespoon instant minced onions
> ½ teaspoon dried dill weed, rosemary,
>   or other herb
> Melted butter
> Salt

Scald milk, remove from heat, and stir in sugar, salt, and butter until dissolved. Cool to lukewarm. In a large bowl, dissolve yeast in the warm water. Add cooled milk mixture. Stir flour into yeast mixture. Add instant minced onions and dill or other

herb; stir all together until well blended, about 2 minutes. Cover and let rise in warm place until tripled in bulk, about 45 minutes. Stir down, and beat vigorously about ½ minute. Turn into a greased 8-inch cake pan or 9-inch pie pan. Bake in a moderate oven (350°) about 1 hour. Brush top crust with melted butter and sprinkle lightly with salt. Cool on rack. Makes one 8-inch loaf.

PIMIENTO CHEESE BREAD

Herbs—marjoram and thyme—add to the good flavor of this yeast bread. The amount of pimiento is not large, but it makes a good show.

> About 3¾ cups regular all-purpose
>   flour (sift before measuring)
> 2 tablespoons melted butter
> 1 tablespoon sugar
> 1 teaspoon salt
> ½ teaspoon powdered marjoram
> ¼ teaspoon powdered thyme
> 1 cup milk
> ⅓ cup shredded processed
>   sharp cheese
> ¼ cup finely chopped pimiento
> 1 package yeast, active dry or
>   compressed
> 2 tablespoons warm water (luke-
>   warm for compressed yeast)

Spoon out 3 tablespoons of the flour and blend with butter, sugar, salt, marjoram, and thyme in a medium-sized saucepan over medium heat. Stir in milk. Cook, stirring, until thick and smooth. Remove from heat; add cheese and pimiento; stir until cheese melts; cool to lukewarm.

Soften yeast in the warm water; add to cheese mixture. Then add flour in 2 or 3 portions, beating until smooth after each addition. Mix to a stiff dough (dough will soften slightly upon kneading); turn out on lightly floured board, and knead gently until dough rounds up in a smooth ball. Return to pan, or to greased bowl; grease top; cover with a damp cloth, and let rise in a warm place until almost doubled in bulk, about 50 to 60 minutes.

Punch down on floured board and shape into a

loaf. Place in a greased 9 by 5 by 3-inch loaf pan; cover with a damp cloth and let rise until almost doubled in bulk. Brush with melted butter or shortening. Bake in a moderately hot oven (375°) for 35 minutes. Turn out on a rack and cool completely before storing. Makes 1 loaf.

SWEDISH LIMPA BREAD

The chili-like flavor of cumin seed distinguishes this exceptional loaf of hearty Swedish Rye. This recipe makes 1 giant round loaf or two small ones.

    1 cup boiling water
    ½ cup cracked wheat
    1 teaspoon crushed fennel seed
    1 teaspoon crushed cumin seed
  1½ teaspoons grated orange peel
    2 teaspoons salt
    ⅓ cup molasses
    3 tablespoons shortening
    1 package yeast, active dry or
        compressed
    ¼ cup warm water (lukewarm for
        compressed yeast)
    1 cup milk
    2 cups unsifted rye flour
    About 4½ cups regular all-purpose
        flour (sift before measuring)
    Melted butter

Pour boiling water over cracked wheat, fennel and cumin seed, orange peel, salt, molasses, and

shortening in a large mixing bowl. When cooled to lukewarm, add yeast, dissolved in the ¼ cup warm water. Stir in the milk and rye flour. Add enough all-purpose flour to make a moderately stiff dough. Turn out on lightly floured board and knead about 10 minutes. Place in large greased bowl. Lightly oil top of dough, cover, and set in a warm place to rise until nearly doubled in bulk, about 2 hours. When doubled, punch down; form into 1 large (12-inch) loaf or 2 small (9-inch) round loaves. Place on greased baking sheet.

Allow to rise until almost doubled in bulk, about 1 hour. Place on lower oven shelf to bake. Bake in a moderate oven (350°) 1 hour 15 minutes for 12-inch loaf, 35 minutes for 9-inch loaves. Brush top crusts with melted butter; cool.

HIIVALEIPA (FINNISH BREAD)

The simplicity of this recipe from Finland makes it a good choice for the novice at yeast baking, while the delectability of the bread makes it something the most proficient bread-maker will want to try. The baked loaf is characterized by its textured grain, light brown color, and round shape. The Finnish people usually cut it in wedges, split each wedge, and serve it with butter. It can also be sliced in regular slices.

  1½ cups hot water
    2 tablespoons butter or shortening
    1 tablespoon sugar
    2 teaspoons salt
    1 package yeast, active dry or
        compressed
    ½ cup warm water (lukewarm
        for compressed yeast)
    3 cups whole wheat or rye flour
  2½ cups unsifted regular all-purpose
        flour (or more)
    Melted butter or salad oil

Measure the 1½ cups hot water into a large mixing bowl. Stir in butter, sugar, and salt. Set aside to cool until lukewarm. Meanwhile, dissolve yeast in the ½ cup warm water; leave about 5 minutes, then blend into the first mixture. Stir in

To make Finnish bread, beat dark flour into the yeast mixture, then mix in white flour.

Knead dough on floured board: Push dough forward with heel of hand; fold up with other hand.

Shape dough into two balls, turning edges under to make smooth top. Put on greased baking sheet.

Cut in generous wedges, then split and butter each wedge. Top wedges with jam or honey.

the whole wheat or rye flour; beat with a wooden spoon for about 1 minute. Add 2 cups of all-purpose flour; blend. Turn out on a floured (½ cup flour) board; knead for about 10 minutes (add more flour if necessary), or until the surface is satiny.

Place dough in a greased bowl, brush top with melted butter or salad oil, and cover with a slightly damp cloth. Allow to rise in a warm place until nearly doubled in bulk, about 1 hour.

Punch down and knead lightly; divide dough in half. Shape each half into a round loaf, place on a lightly greased baking sheet, and press down with hands until the dough is about 1 inch thick. Cover and allow to rise about 45 minutes or until nearly doubled. Bake in a hot oven (400°) for 25 to 30 minutes or until crust is light brown. Makes 2 loaves.

BASIC DINNER ROLLS

This is a good basic roll dough that can be shaped into either plain pan rolls or fancy roll shapes such as the eight pictured here. You might want to make a quantity of these and freeze some as described on page 6.

> 1 package yeast, active dry or
>   compressed
> ¼ cup warm water (lukewarm
>   for compressed yeast)
> 2 eggs, plus enough scalded and
>   cooled milk to make 2 cups
>   liquid
> ½ cup (¼ lb.) melted butter
>   or margarine
> 1½ teaspoons salt
> ½ cup sugar
> 6 cups regular all-purpose flour
>   (sift before measuring)

Sprinkle yeast into large bowl; add warm water and stir until dissolved. Add eggs, milk, butter, salt, and sugar, and stir until well blended. Stir in 3 cups of the flour, beating until smooth after each cup is added. Add the fourth cup of flour; beat until dough is smooth and elastic. Stir in the fifth cup of flour to make a stiff dough. Measure the sixth cup of flour and sprinkle about half of it on a board.

Turn the dough out onto the heavily floured board and with well-floured hands knead dough until it is smooth and elastic (about 5 to 7 minutes), using the remaining flour as needed. Place dough in a well-buttered bowl and butter the top lightly. Cover and let rise in a warm place until almost doubled in bulk (1½ to 2 hours).

When dough has almost doubled, punch it down, squeezing the air bubbles out with your hands. Divide dough into four parts, wrap each in plastic film, and refrigerate until chilled. (You can eliminate this last step, but the rolls are much easier to shape with chilled dough.) Using one piece of the chilled dough at a time, shape either plain pan rolls or any of the eight roll shapes shown. To shape pan rolls, pinch off pieces of dough about 1 inch in diameter and form into smooth balls; arrange about 15 balls of dough in

Clover Leaf: Pinch off enough dough for 1-inch balls. Use fingertips to shape each piece, tucking edges under to make smooth tops. Arrange 3 balls in each greased muffin cup.

Parker House: Roll dough ¼ inch thick; cut 2½-inch circles. With dull edge of knife, crease just off center. Brush with butter, fold large part over small; press folded edge firmly.

each greased round or square 8 or 9-inch baking pan, allowing about 1-inch spaces between them. Shape the other dinner rolls as described under each photograph, and arrange either on greased baking sheets or in muffin pans, as indicated. Let rise in a warm place until almost doubled in size. Bake in a hot oven (425°) for about 10 minutes, or until browned.

NOTE: For especially tender-crusted rolls, you can brush the tops with melted butter or margarine before baking; or for crisper-crusted rolls, brush tops with milk, or with 1 egg beaten with 1 tablespoon milk.

Fan Tans: Roll dough to 8 by 15-inch rectangle, ¼ inch thick. Spread with butter; cut into 5 lengthwise strips. Stack evenly; cut in squares. Put in greased pans with a cut side up.

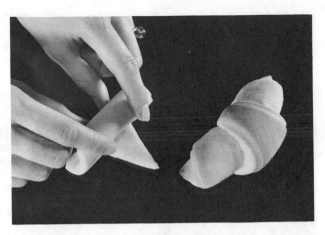

Butterhorns: Roll dough to 8-inch circle, ¼ inch thick. Brush with butter. Cut in wedges; roll each toward point. Place on greased pan, point down. For Crescents, bend into a curve.

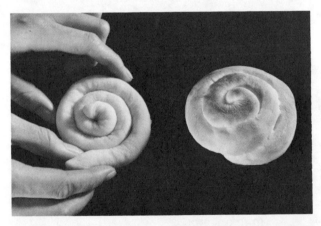

Snails: Roll each piece of dough into a rope about ½ inch in diameter and 10 inches long. Starting at one end, wind strip around and around; tuck outside end firmly underneath.

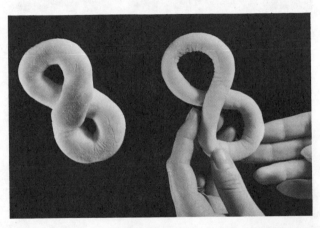

Figure Eights: Roll each piece of dough into a rope about ½ inch in diameter and 10 inches long. Pinch ends together; twist once to form figure 8. Arrange on a greased baking sheet.

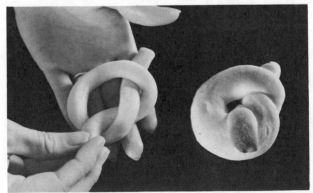

Bowknots: Roll each piece of dough into smooth rope ½ inch in diameter and 9-10 inches long. Gently tie each length once as you would start to make a knot. Place on greased baking pans.

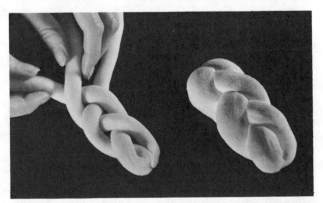

Braids: Form several ropes, each ½ inch in diameter. Braid 3 ropes into a long braid; cut braid into 3½-inch lengths. Pinch together at each end; pull braid slightly to lengthen it.

Sprinkle poppy or sesame seed over bread sticks for an attractive finishing touch.

ITALIAN BREAD STICKS

A combination of salad and olive oils in the dough gives flavor to these bread sticks and is partly responsible for their tender crispness. Extras can be frozen for another meal.

> 1 package yeast, active dry or
> compressed
> ⅔ cup warm water (lukewarm
> for compressed yeast)
> 2 tablespoons salad oil
> 2 tablespoons olive oil
> 1 teaspoon salt
> 1 tablespoon sugar
> About 2¼ cups unsifted regular
> all-purpose flour
> 1 egg, beaten
> Poppy or sesame seed (optional)

Dissolve yeast in the warm water; add salad oil, olive oil, salt, sugar, and 1 cup of the flour. Beat until smooth. Add enough of the remaining flour to make a stiff dough. Turn out on a floured board and knead until smooth and elastic (about 5 minutes), using additional flour as needed. Place

dough in greased bowl, cover with damp towel, and let rise in a warm place until doubled in bulk (about 1 hour).

Punch dough down; divide in half. Cut each half into 24 equal-sized pieces; roll each, using palms of hands, into 6 or 8-inch lengths. Place parallel on greased baking sheets about ½ inch apart. Brush with egg and sprinkle with poppy or sesame seed, if desired. Let rise in warm place until almost doubled (about 30 minutes). Bake in moderately slow oven (325°) for 30 minutes (less for the longer sticks), or until golden. Makes 4 dozen.

WHEAT-NUT ROLLS

Quick-cooking cracked wheat is an unusual ingredient in these rolls.

> ½ cup quick-cooking cracked wheat
> (bulgur)
> 1 cup cold water
> ½ teaspoon salt
> 1 package yeast, active dry or
> compressed
> ¼ cup warm water (lukewarm
> for compressed yeast)
> 1¾ cups milk, scalded and cooled
> to lukewarm
> ½ cup sugar
> ¼ cup salad oil
> 2 teaspoons salt
> 1 egg, slightly beaten
> About 6 cups regular all-purpose
> flour (sift before measuring)

Soak the cracked wheat in the 1 cup cold water and ½ teaspoon salt for several hours or overnight. In a large bowl, dissolve the yeast in the warm water; stir in the scalded and cooled milk, sugar, oil, 2 teaspoons salt, and beaten egg. Add the soaked wheat mixture. Mix in flour to make a stiff dough. Turn out on a floured board and knead until the dough is smooth and elastic.

Place in a greased bowl and let rise in a warm place until almost doubled. Punch down, roll out on a lightly floured board, and cut into any desired roll shapes. Arrange on a greased baking sheet;

let rise in a warm place until almost doubled. Brush tops of rolls lightly with melted butter or salad oil. Bake in a moderately hot oven (375°) for about 15 minutes. Makes about 30 dinner-sized rolls.

CRUSTY WATER ROLLS

These crusty glazed round rolls have a soft, moist interior and a crunchy corn meal bottom crust. To give rolls an extra-crispy crust, place a shallow pan of hot water on the lowest oven shelf; bake rolls below oven center.

*1 cup warm water (lukewarm
    for compressed yeast)
1 tablespoon sugar
1½ teaspoons salt
1 package yeast, active dry or
    compressed
About 3½ cups regular all-purpose
    flour (sift before measuring)
2 tablespoons salad oil
2 egg whites
Corn meal
1 egg yolk
1 tablespoon water*

In a large bowl, stir together the water, sugar, salt, and yeast; stir until yeast is dissolved. Add 1 cup of flour to yeast mixture along with the oil. Beat to a smooth batter. Beat egg whites until stiff but not dry; fold into batter. Add remaining 2½

cups flour and mix to a moderately stiff dough. Turn out on lightly floured board and knead lightly until smooth, about 4 minutes.

Place in greased bowl, cover, and let rise in a warm place until double in bulk, about 1 hour. Punch down, cover, and allow to rise 15 minutes longer. Punch down again, cut dough into 18 pieces. Shape each piece into a ball, dip bottoms in corn meal, place on greased baking sheet, about 1½ inches apart. Cover and let rise until doubled, about 50 minutes. Brush rolls with the egg yolk beaten with the 1 tablespoon water. Bake in a hot oven (400°) for 15 to 20 minutes. Makes 1½ dozen rolls.

RAISED BUTTERMILK BISCUITS

This cross between biscuits and rolls has some of the flavor of each. The crust is tender, with a delicate and even texture.

*1 tablespoon sugar
2 tablespoons warm water (lukewarm
    for compressed yeast)
1 package yeast, active dry or
    compressed
2 cups regular all-purpose flour
    (sift before measuring)
1 teaspoon baking powder
1 teaspoon salt
2 tablespoons shortening
⅔ cup buttermilk*

In a small bowl, mix sugar with the water; add yeast and stir to dissolve. Sift flour again with the baking powder and salt into a large bowl. Cut in the shortening to fine crumb stage, as you would for ordinary biscuits. Add buttermilk and the yeast mixture; mix to a moderately stiff dough. Knead lightly for a few seconds; roll to ½ inch thickness. Cut into biscuits, using a 2 or 2¼-inch biscuit cutter. Arrange in a greased baking pan so biscuits barely touch each other; prick tops with a fork, and brush with melted butter. Let rise in a warm place until almost doubled in bulk, about 30 or 40 minutes. Bake in a hot oven (425°) for 10 to 15 minutes. Makes about 1 dozen.

SOFT PRETZELS

German soft pretzels are crusty, but have a more breadlike interior than commercial pretzels. Although they are best the day you bake them, you can freeze extras in sealed plastic bags and reheat.

Dip the pretzels in a mild lye solution before baking to get the characteristic pretzel flavor and shiny crust. Lye at this low concentration (1 part lye to 64 of water) will not remain on the pretzels in dangerous amounts. Do use caution, however, when working with the solution: When hot it can cause burns.

Keep pretzels from sticking by using baking sheets that have been heated, then rubbed evenly with beeswax or paraffin.

2 packages yeast, active dry or
*   compressed*
¼ cup warm water (lukewarm
*   for compressed yeast)*
1 quart milk
¾ cup soft shortening
½ cup sugar
12 cups unsifted regular all-purpose
*   flour*
1½ teaspoons baking powder
1½ tablespoons salt
2 tablespoons household lye
2 quarts water
3 tablespoons coarse salt

Soften yeast in water. Scald milk; stir in shortening and sugar until shortening is melted. Pour milk mixture into a large bowl and cool until lukewarm. Add softened yeast with 6 cups of the flour and stir until smooth. Cover and let rise in warm place until light and bubbly, about 30 minutes. Sift remaining flour with baking powder and the 1½ tablespoons salt. Stir down risen dough; gradually beat in flour mixture until dough is blended. Let rise, covered, in a greased large bowl until doubled, about 1½ hours.

Punch dough down, divide into 6 equal pieces, and let rest 10 minutes. Divide each piece into 10 portions of equal size. Using palms of hands, roll each into a strand ½ inch in diameter and 18 inches long. Twist into a pretzel shape, tucking ends under. Cover shaped pretzels lightly. When all the dough is shaped, the first pretzels will have risen.

Add lye to cold water in a large pan (do not use an aluminum pan); heat until solution is steaming but not boiling. Place pretzels 1 at a time, right-side down, on a wide slotted turner. Lower pretzel into lye solution for 1 to 2 seconds; remove and drain. Place right-side up on waxed baking sheets; sprinkle with coarse salt. Bake in a hot oven (400°) for 15 minutes or until well browned. Makes 5 dozen 5-inch pretzels.

SALT STICKS

Salt sticks are shaped in the same way as croissants, without the final curve.

2 packages yeast, active dry or
*   compressed*
1 cup warm water (lukewarm
*   for compressed yeast)*
½ cup undiluted evaporated milk
¼ cup sugar
2 teaspoons salt
3 tablespoons salad oil
*   About 3½ cups unsifted regular*
*   all-purpose flour*
1 egg white, slightly beaten
2 tablespoons coarse salt
2 tablespoons caraway seed

Soften yeast in water in a large bowl. Stir in milk, sugar, salt, oil, and 2 cups of the flour. Mix well. Add enough more flour to make a soft dough. Turn out on a lightly floured board and knead until smooth and satiny, about 10 minutes. Place in a greased bowl, cover, and let rise until nearly doubled, about 1 hour.

Punch dough down. Divide dough into 4 equal portions; let rest 10 minutes. Shape each portion into a ball; roll out to a 10-inch circle. Cut each circle of dough into 8 pie-shaped wedges. Beginning at wide end, roll each wedge tightly. Place on greased baking sheets with points under; brush with egg white, then sprinkle with coarse salt and caraway seed. Let rise for 30 minutes. Bake in a hot oven (400°) for 15 minutes or until browned. Makes 32 salt sticks.

For a tasty snack, spread soft pretzels and caraway-seeded salt sticks with butter or German-style mustard.

Pretzels are twisted into characteristic shape from 18-inch strands of yeast dough.

Salt sticks are fashioned from wedges of dough which are rolled up toward pointed end.

BASIC STIR-AND-DROP ROLLS

These tender, light rolls go together quickly because the dough doesn't require kneading or shaping. By augmenting the basic recipe with fruit, nuts, cheese, bacon, chocolate, or spices, you can vary the rolls to complement your menu.

1 package yeast, active dry or
*   compressed*
1 cup warm water (lukewarm
*   for compressed yeast)*
4 tablespoons (¼ cup) sugar
1 teaspoon salt
1 egg, beaten
3 cups regular all-purpose flour
*   (sift before measuring)*
4 tablespoons (¼ cup) salad oil

Dissolve yeast in the warm water; add sugar, salt, and beaten egg. Stir mixture well, then let stand while you sift flour again. Add oil and half of the flour to yeast mixture; beat until very smooth. Add remaining flour to yeast mixture and blend well. Set dough in a warm place and allow to rise until almost doubled in bulk, about 30 minutes.

Drop dough by the spoonful into small greased muffin pans so each cup is half full. Let rise until almost doubled in bulk. Bake in a hot oven (400°) for 15 minutes. Makes 24 rolls.

VARIATIONS (METHOD 1)

After the dough has risen, divide into four parts and place each part in a bowl with one of the ingredients listed below Mix each portion of dough with the added ingredient until well blended. Then proceed with the basic recipe.

¼ cup drained crushed pineapple
4 tablespoons chopped raisins
4 tablespoons finely chopped pecans,
*   walnuts, or almonds*
¼ cup shredded Cheddar cheese
¼ cup crumbled crisp-fried bacon
1 tablespoon cocoa mixed with
*   1 tablespoon sugar*
2 teaspoons cinnamon

VARIATIONS (METHOD 2)

After mixing the basic dough (and after you let it rise), put one of the ingredients listed below in each greased muffin cup. Half fill the prepared cups with the basic dough, let rise until almost doubled in bulk, and bake in a hot oven (400°) for 15 minutes.

1 teaspoon poppy or sesame seed
1 teaspoon butter, 1 teaspoon brown
*   sugar, and 3 pecan halves*
1 teaspoon butter and 1 teaspoon
*   shredded coconut*
1 teaspoon butter and 1 teaspoon jelly

BRAN ROLLS

For yeast rolls containing shredded bran, these are remarkably light and tender.

2 packages yeast, active dry or
*   compressed*
1 cup warm water (lukewarm
*   for compressed yeast)*
1 cup boiling water
1 cup shortening
⅔ cup sugar
1 cup whole bran
1½ teaspoons salt
2 eggs
6 cups regular all-purpose flour
*   (sift before measuring)*

Dissolve yeast in warm water. Pour boiling water over shortening in a mixing bowl; stir in sugar, shredded bran, and salt, and let stand until lukewarm. Beat eggs well and mix into shredded bran mixture; add yeast mixture and mix well.

Mix in flour, 1 cup at a time. Cover and let rise in a warm place until almost doubled, about 2½ hours. Punch down and drop dough by the spoonful into greased muffin pans, filling half full. Let rise until almost doubled, about 1 hour. Bake in a moderately hot oven (375°) for 15 minutes. Makes 48 rolls.

CRANBERRY-PINEAPPLE ROLLS

These flower-shaped yeast rolls have a tart fruit filling of whole cranberry sauce and crushed pineapple.

1 package yeast, active dry or
    compressed
¼ cup warm water (lukewarm
    for compressed yeast)
½ cup milk
1½ tablespoons sugar
½ teaspoon salt
¼ cup (⅛ lb.) butter or margarine
1 egg, beaten
    About 3 cups regular all-purpose
    flour (sift before measuring)
½ cup whole cranberry sauce
¼ cup drained, crushed pineapple
½ teaspoon grated orange peel

Dissolve yeast in the warm water. Scald milk, add sugar, salt, and butter; cool to lukewarm. Mix in dissolved yeast and egg.

Gradually mix in flour. Turn out on a floured board and knead until smooth. Put in a greased bowl, cover, and let rise until almost doubled in bulk.

Roll out dough ¼ inch thick, cut into rounds 1¼ inches in diameter, making 72. Arrange dough rounds in a greased muffin pan, placing 5 rounds around side of each cup and 1 in center. Let rise 30 minutes.

Mix together cranberry sauce, crushed pineapple, and grated orange peel. Punch down center round of each raised roll with a finger and put 1 tablespoon cranberry filling in the middle of each. Bake in a hot oven (400°) for 12 minutes. Makes 12 large rolls.

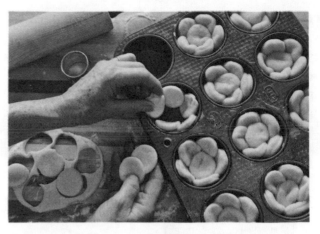

To make Cranberry-Pineapple Rolls, place 5 dough rounds around sides of cups, 1 in center.

Punch down center round of each raised roll and put a tablespoon of filling in the middle.

Rolls come from the oven lightly browned and with the jam already in them.

CROISSANTS

These crescent-shaped, flaky rolls are delicious with any meal, but to serve them in the French manner—freshly baked, for breakfast—you will probably want to start them the day before. You can bake them completely and reheat them the next morning; or, for a totally fresh effect, bake the rolls until they are almost done, cool, keep airtight in the refrigerator (or freeze), then bake in the morning long enough to complete browning.

1 cup (½ lb.) butter
1 package yeast, active dry or
    compressed
¼ cup warm water (lukewarm
    for compressed yeast)
¾ cup milk, scalded and cooled to
    lukewarm
1 tablespoon sugar
½ teaspoon salt
2¾ cups regular all-purpose flour
    (sift before measuring)
1 egg yolk, beaten
1 tablespoon cold milk

Remove the butter from refrigerator and let stand at room temperature while you prepare the

Light, flaky, crisp and hot, these yeast dough croissants are not difficult to make.

yeast dough. Soften yeast in the warm water; blend with lukewarm milk, sugar, and salt. Mix flour into the liquid mixture, stirring until well blended. Turn dough onto a floured board and knead for about 4 minutes or until dough is smooth and elastic.

Rinse mixing bowl with warm water, dry, and butter; place dough in bowl. Cover and let rise in a warm place until doubled in bulk (takes about 2 hours). Punch dough down and knead several turns to expel most of the air bubbles.

Roll on a floured board to form a large rectangle about ¼ inch thick. Cut butter in slices (it should be just soft enough to spread on a firm bread, but not meltingly soft) and arrange in the center ⅓ section of the dough rectangle. Fold each extending side over the butter, pressing together the open edges to seal. Roll out again on floured board until rectangle is about ⅜ inch thick; turn dough occasionally, flouring board lightly to prevent sticking. Fold in thirds again to make a squarish rectangle. Roll dough and fold again in exactly the same manner.

Wrap dough in waxed paper or foil and chill for 15 to 30 minutes. If at any time dough oozes butter and becomes sticky while you're rolling it, chill until butter is firmer. Roll and fold again two more times exactly as directed before. Chill dough again, wrapped in waxed paper or foil, for 15 to 30 minutes.

Roll dough into a rectangle that is ⅛ inch thick. Cut in triangles approximately 6 inches on narrow side and 8 inches on 2 remaining sides. Roll up each triangle of dough from 6-inch edge, pinching tip securely to middle section of roll. Shape each roll into a crescent (tighter than a half circle) and place on an ungreased baking sheet with the sealed point down; allow about a 1½-inch space around all sides of crescents.

Cover lightly and let rise in a warm, draft-free place. When about doubled in bulk (takes about 2 hours), brush each roll gently with mixture of beaten egg yolk and cold milk. Bake in a moderately hot oven (375°) for 25 minutes or until golden brown. Serve hot or reheat in a moderate oven (350°) for about 8 minutes. (Croissants served in Paris are usually a deeper brown than we bake rolls. If you want to duplicate the French style, bake the croissants 5 to 7 minutes longer.) Makes about 18 croissants.

To prepare croissants for final baking later, bake in a moderately hot oven (375°) for 18 minutes. Cool on wire racks and package airtight. Refrigerate for as long as 2 days, or freeze (thaw to bake). Just before serving, complete the baking in a moderately hot oven (375°) for 12 to 15 minutes or until rolls are a golden brown.

YEAST HONEY BUNS

Credit the tender, moist quality of these fluffy buns to the honey and the fresh mashed potatoes. Shape the dough into small pan rolls, and serve them with marmalade for tea or for brunch. Or try them split and toasted, like small versions of English muffins.

> *1 package yeast, active dry or*
> *   compressed*
> *¼ cup warm water or potato water*
> *   (lukewarm for compressed yeast)*
> *3 tablespoons milk or water*
> *⅓ cup salad oil*
> *⅓ cup honey*
> *½ cup lukewarm, freshly cooked,*
> *   sieved potatoes (no seasoning*
> *   or milk added)*
> *1½ teaspoons salt*
> *1 egg, beaten*
> *   About 3 cups regular all-purpose*
> *   flour (sift before measuring)*
> *   Melted butter*

Dissolve yeast in the warm water. Combine milk, salad oil, honey, potatoes, and salt. Add egg, then the yeast mixture. Add flour to honey mixture, mixing to make a soft, but not sticky, dough. Knead on lightly floured board until surface of dough is smooth and small blisters appear just under surface. Place in greased bowl, cover with a damp cloth, and let rise until double in bulk, about 1½ hours.

Shape into rolls, and place in a greased baking pan (about 12 by 17 inches). Let rise until double in bulk, about 45 minutes. Brush with melted butter. Bake in a hot oven (425°) for 12 to 15 minutes. Makes about 3 dozen small rolls.

BASIC BRIOCHE DOUGH

There are many techniques and recipes for making brioche. The one we give here satisfies all the requirements of good brioche: The dough contains ample butter and lots of eggs; it bakes golden throughout; the texture is even, light, and springy; the crust is a crisp brown. Following this basic recipe are recipes for shaping the brioche dough into 5 classic shapes, and for baking it in standard loaf pans.

This brioche dough is no more complicated than any yeast dough. Two pointers, however, will help ensure success: (1) Be prepared to do some energetic hand mixing if you don't have a fairly heavy-duty electric mixer; (2) Chill dough thoroughly before shaping—a minimum of four hours—to make the rich dough firm enough to handle.

> *2 packages yeast, active dry or*
> *   compressed*
> *¼ cup warm water (lukewarm*
> *   for compressed yeast)*
> *½ cup plus 1 tablespoon milk*
> *1 tablespoon sugar*
> *2 teaspoons salt*
> *4½ cups regular all-purpose flour*
> *   (sift before measuring)*
> *1 cup (½ lb.) soft butter*
> *5 eggs*
>
> GLAZE:
> *1 egg yolk*
> *1 tablespoon milk*

In a large bowl blend yeast with warm water until dissolved. Stir in milk (previously heated to scalding, then cooled), sugar, and salt. With heavy-duty electric mixer or a sturdy spoon, beat 2 cups of the flour into yeast mixture; add soft butter and continue beating until blended. Add remaining flour and the eggs, one at a time, beating thoroughly with each addition. At this point, the dough will be soft and sticky. Continue beating until dough is shiny and elastic, about 10 minutes at medium speed with a heavy-duty mixer, about 20 minutes by hand using this technique: Grab the dough with your hands and pull it out of the bowl, then vigorously slap or throw it back into

Strenuous mixing gives breads made of brioche dough their feathery light, springy texture.

Petites Brioches: Smooth top of dough by pulling surface to under side. Add a topknot.

the bowl; continue until dough begins to pull away from your hands.

Cover bowl and set in a warm place until dough is about doubled in bulk, from 2 to 4 hours. Stir dough thoroughly. Cover and refrigerate overnight. Make glaze by combining egg yolk and milk. Form, glaze, and bake the chilled dough as directed in any of the recipes below.

(NOTE: If you want to freeze bread made with brioche dough, first cool the bread thoroughly and then wrap airtight in foil.)

PETITES BRIOCHES
(Little Brioches)

Prepare 1 recipe Basic Brioche Dough. Lightly dust your hands with flour, and then divide the chilled dough into portions of ¼ cup each (measure one portion to get the approximate size), placing them so that they don't touch on a lightly floured baking pan. Cover with waxed paper and place in the refrigerator. Remove 4 or 5 portions of dough at a time to shape; keep remainder cold.

To shape each brioche, pinch off about one-fifth of each individual portion of dough and set aside. Shape the larger section into a smooth ball, pulling the surface of the dough with your thumbs to the underside of the ball. Place ball, smooth side up, in a buttered individual brioche pan or large muffin tin (dough should fill pan half way). Roll the small piece of dough into a tear-drop or pear shape.

Using a sharp pointed knife, cut an X in the exact center of the large ball of dough, and with the floured tip of the knife, poke down the 4 points where the X intersects. Holding the tear-drop-shaped dough by its sides, put it pointed end down into this hole (don't push the top down); place flat side of floured knife against the side of the top-knot and push down gently; repeat all the way around until top-knot is nested in.

Cover shaped brioches lightly with waxed paper and place in a warm place. Let rise until about double, about 2 hours. Carefully brush tops with glaze; it should not run into the joint of the two balls. Bake in a hot oven (425°) for about 20 minutes, or until nicely browned. Remove from pans and serve warm, or allow to cool in pan on wire racks. Makes 18 to 20.

Brioche au Fromage: Knead diced Swiss cheese into brioche dough that has risen once.

Brioche en Couronne: Shape dough into ring by pulling from center hole. Slash top evenly.

BRIOCHE À TETE
(Brioche with a Head)

Prepare 1 recipe Basic Brioche Dough. Pinch off one-fifth of the entire piece of dough, then shape both pieces as directed for Petite Brioche. Place in a large buttered 9-inch-wide brioche mold or a 2-quart round baking pan. Cover with waxed paper; place in a warm spot until about doubled in bulk, about 2 hours. Brush with egg yolk and milk glaze. Bake in a moderate oven (350°) for about 1 hour or until well browned and a wooden skewer comes out clean when inserted. Cool in pan on wire rack, or serve warm.

BRIOCHE AU FROMAGE

Knead ½ pound (2 cups) finely diced Swiss cheese into 1 recipe Basic Brioche Dough. Shape any of the ways suggested and place in or on very well-buttered pans; cover and let rise, then bake as directed for the particular shape you used.

BRIOCHE EN COURONNE
(Crown Brioche)

Prepare 1 recipe Basic Brioche Dough. Shape the chilled dough into one round flat cake about 2 inches thick; place on a greased baking sheet. Form into a ring by piercing dough in the center, then pulling the dough apart evenly, keeping your hands opposite each other and tucking the torn edges under as you go. Make center hole about 5½ inches in diameter. Lightly slash around the top of the ring at 1½-inch intervals. Cover lightly with waxed paper and place in a warm spot until almost doubled in size, about 2 hours. Brush gently with the egg yolk and milk glaze. Bake in a hot oven (400°) for about 35 to 40 minutes, or until ring is well browned and a wooden skewer comes out clean when inserted. Serve warm or cold, sliced.

(NOTE: You can make 2 small crown brioches by dividing dough in half and shaping it into flat round cakes about 1½ inches thick. Make center hole 4½ inches in diameter. Bake as directed for the full-sized crown brioche, but decrease baking time to about 30 minutes.)

Raisin Spice Bagels make a tasty breakfast bread. Serve them hot with butter or whipped cream cheese.

BRIOCHE LOAVES

One recipe Basic Brioche Dough will make 2 regular loaves 5 by 9 inches, or 4 small loaves about 2½ by 5 inches. Bake in a moderately hot oven (375°), allowing 50 minutes for large loaves, 35 minutes for small loaves. Serve warm or let cool in pan on wire rack.

EGG BAGELS

These doughnut-shaped yeast rolls are boiled before they are baked. They're good plain; or you can split and toast them, and spread with butter

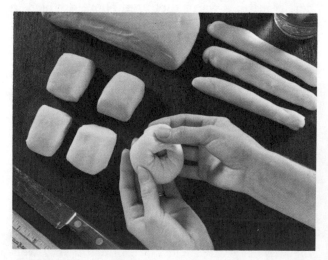

Boil bagels for 3 minutes, then remove them with a slotted spoon and bake.

or cream cheese. Use bagels for sandwich rolls, open-faced or closed—the classic combination is cream cheese and lox (smoked salmon).

>   2 packages yeast, active dry or
>   compressed
>   2 cups warm potato water (lukewarm
>   for compressed yeast)
>   4 eggs
>   1 tablespoon salt
>   1 tablespoon sugar
>   ¼ cup salad oil
>   About 8 cups unsifted regular
>   all-purpose flour
>   Sugar
>   Boiling water
>   2 egg yolks beaten with
>   2 tablespoons water

Soften yeast in ½ cup of the potato water (water in which peeled potatoes have been cooked). Beat eggs in large bowl; blend in the softened yeast, remaining potato water, salt, sugar, oil, and 2 cups of the flour. Stir in remaining flour to make a soft dough.

Turn out on a lightly floured board and knead for about 10 minutes, adding more flour as needed to make a firm dough. Place the dough in a greased bowl, cover lightly, and let rise in a warm place until doubled in bulk.

Punch the dough down, and knead it for a few minutes on a lightly floured board until it is smooth. Roll the dough out to a rectangle, and divide into 32 pieces of equal size. Roll each piece between the palms to form a strand about 6 inches long and ¾ inch in diameter. Moisten the ends, and seal them together firmly to make doughnut-shaped rolls of uniform thickness. Let them rise on board for about 15 minutes (if the rolls come unsealed during rising, reseal ends before boiling).

Dissolve 2 tablespoons of sugar in 2 quarts of boiling water in a deep pot. Drop bagels into the water, one at a time. They will rise quickly to the surface. Do not crowd. As the bagels come to the surface, turn them over. Boil for 3 minutes on the second side. Remove with slotted or runcible spoon and place on greased baking sheets; brush with egg yolk glaze. Bake in a hot oven (425°) for 20 to 25 minutes, or until the crust is golden brown and crisp. Makes 32 bagels.

ALMOND RAISIN BAGELS

Follow recipe for Egg Bagels, but along with the first addition of flour, stir in 1 cup finely chopped blanched almonds, 2 cups golden raisins, and 2 teaspoons grated lemon peel.

RAISIN SPICE BAGELS

Increase the sugar in Egg Bagel recipe to ¼ cup. Sift 2 teaspoons cinnamon, 1 teaspoon nutmeg, and ½ teaspoon cardamom with part of the flour, and add 1 cup seedless raisins.

RYE BAGELS

In Egg Bagel recipe, substitute 3 cups of rye flour for 3 cups of the regular all-purpose flour, increase salt to 2 tablespoons, and add 2 tablespoons grated orange peel and 2 tablespoons caraway seed. Sprinkle bagels with caraway seed before baking, pressing the seeds firmly down into the dough.

ONION BAGELS

Add ½ cup instant toasted onions to Egg Bagel dough; after brushing with egg yolk, sprinkle rolls with poppy seed and additional instant toasted onions, if you wish, pressing onions in firmly.

SWEET YEAST BREADS

Tender and richly flavored, and beautiful to look at, these sweet rolls and breads are delicious with coffee or afternoon tea. Some of them are dressed up with fillings, glazes, or toppings; others are baked in fancy molds, or folded or twisted into intriguing shapes. Bake these breads when you want to serve something special.

Some of these recipes make more than one loaf, or a quantity of rolls. You can freeze the extras after they are baked, or if you wish, you can freeze the unbaked loaves or rolls for a short period (see *How to freeze unbaked bread dough* on page 6).

Although some of the molded breads have their special, traditional shapes, you can bake them successfully in any mold you choose (including metal salad molds). Season the mold if it is new or has never been greased before. To do this, heavily grease the mold with a hydrogenated shortening or lard, then place it in a 300° oven for 1 hour, or until it begins to smoke. Remove from oven and let cool. With paper towels, wipe out the excess shortening. Butter the mold as directed in the recipe before you bake in it, and fill the mold no more than half full (bake any excess batter in another mold or baking tin). Let bread cool in the mold (do not invert) at least 15 minutes before turning. As the bread cools, the texture becomes firm enough for it to support its own weight. If you use a heavy baking mold that cools slowly, let it cool until you can comfortably hold the mold in your hand; this may take up to an hour.

A colorful basket of Easter breads:
Hot Cross Buns, page 56; Filled Buns,
page 48; Glazed Lemon Buns, page 49.

BASIC SWEET DOUGH

This sweet dough is soft—about as soft as you can handle without having it stick to your hands or the board when kneading. It makes very light, tender breads and, because it is rich, it doesn't require much kneading—just enough to work about ¼ to ½ cup flour into the dough for easy handling.

> ¼ cup (⅛ lb.) butter or margarine
> 1 teaspoon salt
> ¼ cup sugar
> 1 cup milk, scalded and cooled to lukewarm
> 1 package yeast, active dry or compressed
> ¼ cup warm water (lukewarm for compressed yeast)
> 1 egg, slightly beaten
> About 4 cups regular all-purpose flour (sift before measuring)
> Softened butter

Place the butter, salt, and sugar in a large bowl; add the lukewarm milk, stirring to dissolve the sugar and salt and to melt the butter. Soften the yeast in the warm water and add, along with the beaten egg, to the milk mixture. Stir in 3½ cups of the flour, 1 cup at a time, beating vigorously to blend. Scrape dough from the sides of the bowl and brush the top of the dough and the sides of the bowl with softened butter. Cover dough and let rise in a warm place about 2 hours, or until almost doubled in bulk. Then turn out on a well-floured board and knead lightly, adding flour until the dough is no longer sticky (do not use more than ¼ to ½ cup flour on the board). Shape and bake as suggested in the recipes that follow.

BUBBLE RING

Balls of dough are layered in a tube pan to make this unusual bread. The balls break off into individual rolls for serving.

> 1 recipe Basic Sweet Dough
>   (page 33)
> ½ to ¾ cup chopped nuts
>   About ½ cup (¼ lb.)
>   melted butter

GLAZE:

> ⅓ cup dark corn syrup
> 2 tablespoons melted butter
> ½ teaspoon vanilla

Pinch off pieces of the Basic Sweet Dough and with your fingertips shape each piece into a smooth ball about 1 inch in diameter, tucking the edges under to make a smooth top. Place one layer of balls, about ½ inch apart, in a well-buttered 10-inch tube pan. Brush with about ⅓ of the melted butter and sprinkle with ⅓ of the chopped nuts. Arrange two more layers, placing balls over the spaces in the layer below, topping each layer with melted butter and nuts. Let dough rise in a warm place until almost doubled in bulk. Bake in a moderate oven (350°) for 35 to 40 minutes.

Make glaze by mixing together the corn syrup, 2 tablespoons melted butter, and the vanilla. Pour glaze over the bubble ring after it is baked. Let the ring stand for about 10 minutes before removing it from the pan.

FOUR-LAYERED APPLE COFFEE CAKE

The Basic Sweet Dough recipe on page 33 makes two of these coffee cakes. You can freeze one of them unbaked to use another time; or use half of the dough to make ½ recipe of Glazed Orange rolls or Cinnamon Rolls (page 35).

> 1 recipe Basic Sweet Dough
>   (page 33)
> 1½ cups brown sugar, firmly packed
> 1½ cups chopped nuts
> ⅓ cup flour
> 1 tablespoon cinnamon
>   Dash each nutmeg and cloves
> ⅓ cup melted butter

FOR EACH COFFEE CAKE:

> 4 to 6 tablespoons softened butter
> 4 to 5 tablespoons raisins or currants
> 1 medium-sized apple, peeled and
>   chopped

Prepare a streusel mixture of the brown sugar, chopped nuts, flour, cinnamon, nutmeg, cloves, and the ⅓ cup melted butter. Roll out ½ of the sweet dough on a lightly floured board to a 16-inch square. Spread ½ of the square with 1 to 2 tablespoons softened butter and sprinkle with ¾ cup of the streusel mixture. Spread 2 to 3 tablespoons of the raisins or currants and about ¾ of the chopped apple over the streusel. Fold the plain half of the dough over the filling.

Spread half of the rectangle with 1 to 2 tablespoons softened butter and sprinkle with about ½ cup streusel, about 2 tablespoons raisins or currants, and the remaining chopped apple. Fold over dough to form an 8-inch square. Pinch edges of dough together to seal in filling. Place in a well-buttered 8 or 9-inch square pan. Spread top with about 2 tablespoons softened butter and sprinkle with ½ cup streusel. (Coffee cake may be frozen at this point, wrapped in plastic film or foil.) Let rise in a warm place until almost doubled in bulk. Bake in a moderate oven (350°) for about 35 minutes. Repeat steps to make a second coffee cake. (To use frozen coffee cake, remove from freezer, unwrap, and set in a warm place for about 3 to 3½ hours to thaw and rise before baking.)

GLAZED ORANGE ROLLS

Serve these rolls warm "as is" or topped with an orange glaze.

> 1 recipe Basic Sweet Dough
>   (page 33)
> ½ cup (¼ lb.) softened butter
> 1 cup sugar
>   Grated peel of 2 medium-sized
>   oranges

ORANGE GLAZE:
> ½ cup sugar
> ¼ cup light corn syrup
> ¼ cup water
>   Grated peel of 1 orange

Roll out Basic Sweet Dough to a rectangle about ¼ inch thick. Cream together the butter, 1 cup sugar, and grated peel of the 2 oranges. Spread mixture evenly over the dough. Roll dough up as for a jelly roll and chill. Cut chilled dough into 1-inch slices, and place in greased muffin pans or 1 inch apart on greased baking sheets. (Those baked in muffin cups will be tall and those baked on baking sheets will be larger and flatter.) Allow rolls to rise in a warm place until almost doubled in bulk. Bake in a hot oven (425°) for 10 to 14 minutes. While still warm, top with orange glaze. Makes about 2 dozen rolls.

To make the orange glaze, simmer together the ½ cup sugar, corn syrup, and water for about 10 minutes; add the grated peel of the 1 orange. Cool syrup slightly before glazing the warm rolls.

INSIDE-OUT CINNAMON ROLLS

These cinnamon rolls have the brown sugar mixture on the outside. These start with the Basic Sweet Dough on page 33.

Roll out 1 recipe of Basic Sweet Dough (page 33) to a large rectangle, about 10 by 24 inches and ¼ inch thick; spread with softened butter (about 3 tablespoons). Sprinkle with ¾ cup brown sugar and about 2 teaspoons cinnamon. Cut into strips about 10 inches long and 1 inch wide,

and roll each separately into a snail shape, with the sugar side out.

Place rolls 1 inch apart on a greased baking sheet and sprinkle tops with the excess sugar that fell off the dough. Let rolls rise in a warm place until almost doubled in bulk. Bake in a moderate oven (350°) for 20 to 25 minutes. Makes about 2 dozen rolls.

REFRIGERATOR SWEET YEAST DOUGH

Here is a sweet yeast refrigerator dough that allows you to stop midway in your bread making and complete the process in less than 2 hours another day. It is necessary that this dough be refrigerated for 3 hours or more after it has risen and been punched down. At that stage, you wrap the dough securely in plastic film to chill. You can then store it in the refrigerator for as long as three or four days. Whatever the storage period, you must have the dough well chilled in order to work with it.

> 2 packages yeast, active dry or
>   compressed
> ¼ cup warm water (lukewarm
>   for compressed yeast)
> 1¾ cups milk
> ¼ cup sugar
> 1½ cups (¾ lb.) soft butter
> ½ teaspoon salt
> 4 eggs, slightly beaten
> 8 cups unsifted regular all-purpose
>   flour

Soften yeast in the warm water. Scald milk; add sugar and ½ cup (¼ lb.) of the butter, stirring until the butter melts. Cool to lukewarm; stir in the softened yeast and salt. Beat the milk mixture into the eggs to blend well. Place flour in a large bowl; mix in the egg and milk mixture, stirring until the liquid is well blended into the flour and the mixture forms a ball. Knead the dough on a floured board for about 5 minutes, kneading in about ¼ cup more flour as necessary, until dough is smooth and elastic. Let rest for 5 minutes.

Roll out dough to a ¼-inch-thick rectangle, about 12 by 36 inches. Spread about ⅓ cup of the remaining butter over the center third of the dough; fold the right third of the dough over the buttered section and spread ⅓ cup of the remaining butter over that surface. Fold the left third of the dough over the buttered section. Give the folded dough a quarter turn, and roll it again into a rectangle, about ½ inch thick. Spread the center third of the rectangle with the remaining ⅓ cup butter; bring the ends of the rectangle to meet in the center, then fold in half, bringing the edges together. Place dough in a greased bowl, cover, and let rise in a warm place until almost doubled, about 1 hour. Punch dough down, wrap in plastic film, and chill for at least 3 hours or overnight.

Use dough to make Cinnamon Rolls, or use a portion of the dough for a swirled Cinnamon and Raisin Loaf (recipes for both follow). If you wish, you can bake just a quarter of the dough at a time, keeping the remainder refrigerated.

CINNAMON AND RAISIN LOAF FROM REFRIGERATOR DOUGH

You can bake four of these loaves from the recipe for refrigerator dough on page 35, or make just one loaf and use the rest of the dough for the Cinnamon Rolls.

1 recipe Refrigerator Sweet Yeast
Dough (page 35)
½ cup (¼ lb.) melted butter
2 cups seedless or golden raisins
1 cup finely chopped nuts (optional)
1 cup sugar
1 tablespoon cinnamon
Melted butter
Powdered sugar

Divide dough into four equal parts; work with one part at a time, keeping remainder in the refrigerator. Roll out each piece of dough about ¼ inch thick to a rectangle 8 by 16 inches. Spread with 2 tablespoons of the melted butter, then sprinkle dough evenly with ½ cup raisins and ¼

cup chopped nuts (if used). Combine sugar with cinnamon. Sprinkle dough with ¼ of the cinnamon-sugar mixture. Beginning with the narrow side, roll up tightly, sealing the ends and bottom. Place in a greased 9¼ by 5¼-inch loaf pan, cover, and let rise until dough is within ½ inch of the top of the pan, about 1½ hours. Bake in a moderately hot oven (375°) for 30 to 35 minutes or until well browned. Brush with melted butter while hot; sprinkle with powdered sugar. Repeat steps to make a total of 4 loaves.

CINNAMON ROLLS FROM REFRIGERATOR DOUGH

This recipe makes about five dozen cinnamon rolls of extraordinary lightness. You can freeze those you don't use.

1 recipe Refrigerator Sweet Yeast
Dough (page 35)
½ cup (¼ lb.) melted butter
1 cup sugar
1 tablespoon cinnamon
GLAZE *(for each pan of rolls):*
1½ tablespoons warm water
1 cup sifted powdered sugar

Divide refrigerator dough into 8 equal-size pieces. Work with one at a time, returning remaining dough to refrigerator. Roll each piece of the dough out on a floured board to a rectangle about 9 by 12 inches. Brush about 1 tablespoon of the melted butter on the dough. Combine sugar with cinnamon. Sprinkle about 2 tablespoons of the cinnamon-sugar mixture over butter. Roll dough as for a jelly roll, starting with the 12-inch side; seal edge. Cut the roll into eight 1½-inch slices. Place 16 slices, cut sides up, in a greased 8-inch square pan (you will need ¼ of the dough to fill pan), with rolls ½ inch apart.

Let rise until rolls are nearly doubled in size, about 45 minutes. Bake in a moderately hot oven (375°) for 20 to 25 minutes or until well browned. Cool slightly and glaze each pan of rolls with a mixture of the warm water and powdered sugar. Makes 5 dozen 2-inch rolls.

Cinnamon rolls and a swirled raisin loaf are both made from recipe for rich refrigerator dough on page 35.

Spread second addition of butter over folded refrigerator dough.

Final fold: Bring ends of dough to meet in center, then fold in half.

For cinnamon rolls, roll up like jelly roll; cut in 1½-inch slices.

CALIFORNIA COFFEE CAKE

Hot roll mix and a simple marmalade and raisin filling make this coffee cake very easy and quick to prepare.

> 1 package (14 oz.) hot roll mix
> 1 cup orange marmalade
> ½ cup dark raisins, coarsely chopped
> ½ teaspoon ground cloves

Prepare hot roll mix as directed on package. Let rise once. On a lightly floured board roll dough into rectangle about 10 by 20 inches. Spread with a mixture of marmalade, raisins, and cloves. Roll jelly-roll fashion from one of the long sides. Shape into a ring on a greased baking sheet, seam side down. Slash top at 1-inch intervals with scissors. Set in a warm place and cover with waxed paper. Let rise for 40 minutes. Bake in a moderately hot oven (375°) for 20 minutes. Glaze warm cake, if you wish, with ¾ cup sifted powdered sugar blended with 1½ tablespoons water. Slice and serve hot or cooled. Makes 10 servings.

COCONUT COFFEE RINGS

This yeast bread is rich with butter and eggs. The recipe makes three rings. You may want to serve one fresh from the oven and freeze the other two.

> 1 package yeast, active dry or
>   compressed
> 4 tablespoons sugar
> ¼ cup warm water (lukewarm
>   for compressed yeast)
> 3½ cups regular all-purpose flour
>   (sift before measuring)
> 1 teaspoon salt
> ½ cup (¼ lb.) butter or margarine
> 3 egg yolks, well beaten
> 1 cup light cream
> ½ cup powdered sugar
> 1½ tablespoons milk
>   About ½ cup flaked coconut or
>   chopped nuts

Stir yeast and 2 tablespoons of sugar into water. Sift flour again with salt and remaining sugar into a bowl. Cut butter into flour with pastry blender or two knives. Blend egg yolks with cream; stir into flour mixture. Add yeast mixture; blend well. Chill, covered, for several hours.

Divide dough into 6 equal pieces; roll each on floured board into a 12-inch-long rope. Twist each 2 ropes together, pinching ends together into a ring; repeat to make 3 rings. Place each ring on a buttered pie pan; let rise 2 hours, or until nearly doubled.

Bake in a moderate oven (350°) about 30 minutes. While warm, ice top with powdered sugar icing made by blending the ½ cup powdered sugar with the 1½ tablespoons milk. Sprinkle with coconut or nuts.

CARDAMOM COFFEE CAKE

You bake this richly flavored coffee cake in one large (10-cup) mold.

> 1 package yeast, active dry or
>   compressed
> ¼ cup warm water (lukewarm
>   for compressed yeast)
> ¾ teaspoon salt
> ¾ cup sugar
> 1 teaspoon crushed cardamom
> 1 cup milk, scalded and cooled to
>   lukewarm
> 4 eggs
> 4 cups regular all-purpose flour
>   (sift before measuring)
> ½ cup (¼ lb.) butter or margarine,
>   melted and cooled

Dissolve yeast in water in the large bowl of your electric mixer. Add the salt, sugar, cardamom, milk, and eggs, and beat until blended. Add flour gradually to the milk mixture, beating at low speed until batter is smooth. Add butter, and mix until blended.

Butter a large (10-cup) baking mold, or two smaller molds (5 or 6-cup size) and sprinkle with sugar, turning pan so that all sides are covered.

For an airy, coarse-textured coffee cake, turn the batter immediately into the buttered mold and let rise as directed below.

For a fine-textured coffee bread, cover bowl lightly and let batter rise in a warm place until doubled, about 2 hours. Beat batter down and turn into the buttered mold to rise.

Let rise in a warm place until batter comes to ¼ inch from the top of the pan. Bake in a moderate oven (350°) for 65 to 70 minutes for tubeless, 10-cup mold. Bake at 375° for 45 to 50 minutes if you use 5 or 6-cup tubeless molds, or for 35 to 40 minutes in small molds with tubes. Bake until cake tester comes out clean. Let cool in pan before turning out. Makes about 12 servings.

GOLDEN SAFFRON COFFEE BREAD

This coffee bread has an airy texture. Bake it in a 10-cup mold with a tube.

1 package yeast, active dry or
*   compressed*
¼ cup warm water (lukewarm
*   for compressed yeast)*
½ cup milk, scalded and cooled to
*   lukewarm*
$\frac{1}{16}$ teaspoon powdered saffron
1 teaspoon salt
¼ cup sugar
6 eggs
3 cups regular all-purpose flour
*   (sift before measuring)*
½ cup (¼ lb.) butter or margarine,
*   melted and cooled*

Dissolve yeast in the warm water in large bowl of your electric mixer. Add the cooled milk, saffron, salt, sugar, and eggs; beat at low speed until blended. Add flour gradually to the milk mixture, beating until very smooth. With mixer at low speed, blend in the butter or margarine. Cover bowl lightly and let rise in a warm place about 2 hours or until doubled.

Stir dough down then beat well. Spoon into a well-greased 10-cup mold with tube. Cover and let rise in a warm place about 30 minutes, or until almost doubled. Bake in a moderately hot oven (375°) for 50 to 60 minutes, or until golden brown and cake tester comes out clean. Let cool in pan before turning out. Makes about 12 servings.

RUSSIAN NUT BUNS

Hot roll mix shortens the traditional method for making these sweet yeast buns.

2 cups sliced or coarsely chopped
*   almonds*
½ can (15-oz. size) sweetened
*   condensed milk*
¼ cup (⅛ lb.) butter
2 tablespoons milk
⅓ cup raisins
1 package (14 oz.) hot roll mix, or
*   sweet yeast dough for 1 bread*
*   loaf*
2 or 3 tablespoons soft butter
1 cup sifted powdered sugar
4 teaspoons lemon juice
¼ teaspoon almond extract

Combine in a saucepan chopped almonds, sweetened condensed milk, butter, milk. Bring to a boil, stirring. Reduce heat and simmer, stirring, until mixture has a glaze-like appearance, about 5 minutes. Remove from heat, add raisins; let cool.

Make up hot roll mix as directed on package. After it has risen, punch down; on lightly floured board, roll dough into a rectangle about 15 by 20 inches. Spread evenly with butter, then with filling. Roll up, starting with 20-inch side. Cut into 18 slices. Place on well-greased pan, 9 by 13 inches. Cover and let rise in a warm place until about doubled.

Bake in a moderately hot oven (375°) for 20 to 25 minutes or until brown. Turn onto another baking sheet, then turn top side up on a wire rack to cool. While warm, drizzle with an icing made by blending the powdered sugar with lemon juice and almond extract. Makes 1½ dozen nut buns.

NOTE: If you prefer to make this into a single bread loaf, shape the dough into a 9 by 12-inch rectangle, spread with filling, roll up, and place in 5 by 9-inch loaf pan. Let rise. Bake in a moderate oven (350°) for 45 minutes or until browned. Turn out of pan and cool on wire rack. Glaze with icing before it cools.

ORANGE-NUT CRESCENTS

You fill squares of this sweet roll dough with chopped maraschino cherries and pecan meats; when rolled and baked, the pink filling peeks out of both ends of the orange-frosted rolls.

> 1 package yeast, active dry or
>   compressed
> ¼ cup warm water (lukewarm
>   for compressed yeast)
> 4 cups regular all-purpose flour
>   (sift before measuring)
> 3 tablespoons sugar
> 1¼ teaspoons salt
> 1 cup (½ lb.) butter or margarine
> 3 eggs, separated
> ¾ cup milk, scalded and cooled
>   to lukewarm
> ⅓ cup sugar
> ¾ cup finely chopped pecans
> 1 tablespoon grated orange peel
> ¼ cup finely chopped maraschino
>   cherries
> Orange frosting (recipe follows)

Dissolve yeast in the warm water. Sift flour again with sugar and salt into a mixing bowl; cut in the butter with a pastry blender. Beat egg yolks until

thick and stir in the milk and the yeast mixture; combine with the flour mixture and mix thoroughly. Refrigerate overnight.

Roll out half the dough into a large square about ⅛ inch thick, then cut into 3-inch squares. Beat egg whites until stiff, then gradually beat in sugar; fold in nuts, orange peel, and cherries. Place 1 teaspoon of filling in the center of each square. Starting at one corner, roll dough over filling and twist ends around to form a crescent.

Place on a greased baking sheet, with the lapped-over end up. Repeat with the remainder of the dough. Cover and let rise 1 hour, or until almost doubled in bulk. Bake in a moderately hot oven (375°) for 15 minutes. While warm, spread with orange frosting. Makes 4½ dozen.

ORANGE FROSTING: Blend together 2 tablespoons melted butter, 3 tablespoons orange juice, 1 teaspoon grated orange peel, and 1½ cups powdered sugar. Stir in ¼ cup finely chopped pecans.

BROWN SUGAR-LEMON SPINDLE ROLLS

If you crowd yeast rolls, made of very thin layers of dough, into a smaller than usual pan, they squeeze together and pop up into interesting lopsided spirals as they bake.

> 1 package (14 oz.) hot roll mix
> ½ cup (¼ lb.) soft butter
> ¾ cup brown sugar, firmly packed
>   Grated peel of 2 lemons
> 1½ teaspoons cinnamon
> 1 teaspoon mace
> ½ cup water
> 3 tablespoons sugar
>   Dash of cream of tartar

Make sweet yeast dough from hot roll mix, following directions on package. After dough has risen once, punch down. On a lightly floured board, roll out to as thin a layer as possible (a rectangle about 24 by 18 inches). Spread evenly with the soft butter. Sprinkle with a mixture of the brown sugar, grated lemon peel, cinnamon, and mace. Starting with long edge of rectangle, roll dough tightly. Cut into 25 slices (each about 1 inch thick); place cut side up, close together, in a greased 8-inch-square baking pan. Allow to rise in a warm place until almost doubled in bulk, about 40 minutes; bake in a moderately hot oven (375°) for 35 minutes or until brown. (If rolls brown too rapidly, cover with foil during latter part of baking.)

While hot, brush with candy glaze made by boiling together the water, sugar, and cream of tartar until syrup reaches hard crack stage (300°). Makes 25 rolls.

FINNISH COFFEE BRAID

This handsome Finnish braid, rich with eggs and butter, is golden inside and out. Cardamom, which gives the bread its rich fragrance and flavor, is a favorite Scandinavian baking spice, used as liberally and frequently as we use cinnamon. If you buy whole cardamom, discard the white outer pod and use only the seeds. For an additional authentic touch of tradition, sprinkle braids with chopped almonds before baking.

½ cup (¼ lb.) butter
1 package yeast, active dry or
    compressed
3 tablespoons warm water (lukewarm
    for compressed yeast)
2 eggs, beaten
1 cup milk, scalded and cooled
½ cup sugar
½ teaspoon salt
½ teaspoon fresh ground cardamom
    (or finely crushed)
  Grated peel of 1 orange (optional)
  About 5 cups unsifted regular
    all-purpose flour
1 egg yolk
1 tablespoon milk

Melt butter and set aside to cool. Dissolve yeast in the warm water. In a large mixing bowl combine beaten eggs, milk, sugar, salt, cardamom, grated orange peel, yeast mixture, and butter. Stir in enough flour to make a fairly stiff dough. Turn onto a floured board and knead until dough is

Start Finnish Coffee Braid by crossing strands of dough in middle; braid from center to each end.

smooth. Shape into a ball and place in a greased bowl; cover. Put in a warm place and let rise until nearly doubled in bulk, about 2 hours.

Punch down and divide in 2 equal portions (or 3 portions for smaller loaves), then divide each portion into thirds. Roll each third between hands to form strands 18 to 24 inches long (make all the same length), rolling from center. Place 3 strands on a board, crossing in the center, and braid out to each end. Form braid into a ring and pinch ends together. Place on a greased baking sheet. Repeat process to make the second braid. Cover lightly with waxed paper and let rise in a warm place until nearly doubled, from 2 to 2½ hours.

Paint each braid with a mixture of egg yolk beaten with the 1 tablespoon milk. Bake in a moderate oven (350°) for about 45 minutes or until a medium brown. Let cool on wire racks (or serve warm). Decorate if desired. Wrap airtight; to freeze braids, seal in foil. Slice to serve. Makes 2 large loaves or 3 smaller ones.

HUNGARIAN CHEESE-FILLED COFFEE CAKE

Here's a unique creation: a tender, sour cream-yeast bread ring with a center filling of sweetened cream cheese. It is topped with an apricot jam glaze and a fine dusting of powdered sugar.

Unlike many other bread doughs, this one has the egg and yeast mixture added to premeasured dry ingredients. The dough appears soft but is not sticky to handle and knead. Being rich, it develops a fine cakelike texture without lengthy kneading.

The most critical point is the baking. The pastry must bake long enough to set the cheese filling firmly and seal it to the adjacent bread. If under-baked, the center may run or pull away from the bread, leaving a hole. During baking, if the outside crust becomes golden brown too soon, lay a piece of foil loosely on top to keep it from darkening further.

A large 3-quart ring mold is ideal for baking this bread. Lacking such a pan, you may divide the dough in half and shape it into two 9-inch ring molds. Or use a spring form pan with a tube center (place a custard cup upside down in its center if it has a flat bottom).

*2 packages yeast, active dry or
    compressed*
*½ cup warm water (lukewarm
    for compressed yeast)*
1 cup (½ lb.) butter or margarine
*5 cups regular all-purpose flour
    (sift before measuring)*
1¼ cups sugar
½ teaspoon salt
6 egg yolks
1 cup (½ pt.) sour cream
1 large package (8 oz.) cream cheese
2 whole eggs
1 teaspoon vanilla
1 jar (10 oz.) apricot jam
    Powdered sugar

Dissolve yeast in the warm water. Melt butter. Sift flour again with ¾ cup of the sugar and the salt into a large bowl. Beat egg yolks until thick and light; blend in sour cream and melted butter; stir in dissolved yeast. Gradually stir the egg yolk mixture into the dry ingredients, mixing to make a soft, smooth dough. Turn out on a lightly floured board and knead for 5 minutes, or until the dough is smooth. Turn into a bowl, cover, and let rise until almost doubled in bulk.

Meanwhile, prepare cheese filling. Cream the cheese until light and blend in the remaining ½ cup sugar. Add the whole eggs, one at a time, and beat until smooth. Blend in vanilla.

Punch down dough and knead a few minutes. Lightly flour a board; roll out dough into a large circle, about 18 inches in diameter, and lay it over a greased 3-quart ring mold. (If you are using two 9-inch ring molds instead, divide dough in half, and roll each into a circle about 13 inches in diameter.) Fit the dough down into the bottom and sides of the ring mold, being careful not to poke holes in it, and let it hang over the outside. Pour in the cheese filling.

Lift outside edges of dough, and lap over filling; seal to inside ring of dough. Cut a cross in the dough which covers the center of the ring mold and fold each triangle formed back over the ring. Let rise until doubled in bulk (until dough comes up to the top of the pan).

Bake in a moderate oven (350°) for 40 minutes, or until golden brown and a toothpick inserted comes out clean. (If you use two 9-inch ring molds, bake at 350° for 30 minutes.) Let cool for 10 minutes, then turn out with top side down onto a rack.

When bread ring is cool, heat jam until it runs easily; carefully spoon jam over the ring. When set, dust lightly with powdered sugar by shaking about 2 tablespoons sugar through a sieve. To serve, slice the ring in 1-inch wedges. Makes about 2 dozen slices.

Each delicious slice of this tender yeast coffee cake ring has a large center area of cream cheese filling.

Fold dough over filling in mold; seal edges against inner ring.

Cut cross in center, cutting just to rim of the center tube.

Fold back triangles; pinch points securely to dough in pan.

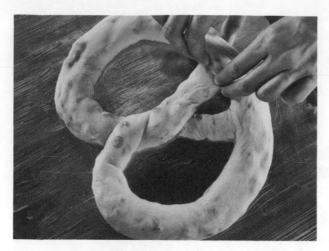

Tuck ends of pretzel-shaped Danish Coffee Ring securely under dough; flatten slightly.

Pine nuts decorate top of cardamom-flavored Danish pastry made from a hot roll mix.

DANISH COFFEE RING

From one package of hot roll mix, you get the basis for two pretzel-shaped, authentic-looking and tasting Danish pastries. However, the method is greatly simplified and much less time consuming than the classic way for making *Wienerbrod* (see pages 50-53).

    1 package (about 14 oz.) hot roll mix
    3 tablespoons sugar
    ½ cup (¼ lb.) soft butter
    ¼ cup unsifted regular all-purpose flour
        Cardamom Butter Filling (recipe follows)
1½ cups golden raisins
    1 egg yolk
    2 teaspoons milk
    ¼ cup sugar
    ½ cup pine nuts or
        sliced, unblanched almonds

Prepare hot roll mix as directed on the package, adding the required ingredients along with the 3 tablespoons sugar. Let rise as directed until almost doubled, then punch down. Wrap in plastic film and chill for about 30 minutes. Cream butter and flour until thoroughly blended. Turn out onto a sheet of waxed paper and cover with a second sheet of waxed paper. Roll out the butter-flour mixture to make a 4 by 10-inch strip; chill for about 30 minutes.

Roll out chilled dough on a floured board to form a 12-inch square. Peel paper from butter and set butter in center of dough. Fold the two wide sides of the dough over butter, then fold in the narrow ends. Fold dough again to make a 5-inch square. Flatten slightly with floured rolling pin, then roll out on floured board to make another 12-inch square; use light strokes to avoid tearing dough. Repeat folding and rolling procedure two more times. Then fold the same way again, wrap dough in plastic film and chill for at least 30 minutes (or as long as 8 hours).

Divide dough in half; rewrap and chill one portion while shaping the other. To make each coffee ring, roll out dough on lightly floured board to make a 6 by 30-inch strip. Spread with half of the cardamom butter filling, leaving ½-inch-wide margin on all sides. Distribute half the raisins evenly over filling. Tightly roll up dough, jelly roll fashion, starting with a 30-inch side; moisten edge to seal. Place roll, seam side down, on a well-greased baking sheet and twist into pretzel shape; tuck ends under roll. Flatten slightly with palm of your hand. Beat egg yolk with milk and brush on shaped dough. Sprinkle with 2 tablespoons of the remaining sugar; top with half the pine nuts, pressing lightly into dough.

Cover rings with waxed paper and a dampened towel (wrung dry); let rise in a warm place for about 30 minutes or until puffy looking. Bake in a moderate oven (350°) for 20 to 25 minutes or until well browned. Cool for about 10 minutes to serve hot, or cool completely on pans. Makes two 10-inch rings.

CARDAMOM BUTTER FILLING: Cream together ½ cup (¼ lb.) soft butter, 2 cups sifted powdered sugar, ¾ teaspoon cardamom, and 3 tablespoons heavy cream or evaporated milk until mixture is fluffy.

NORWEGIAN COFFEE CAKE

Cardamom is the all-pervasive seasoning in this round loaf of yeast bread. It is liberally sprinkled throughout with raisins, citron, and almonds.

    ¾ cup milk
    ⅓ cup shortening
    ½ cup sugar
    1 package yeast, active dry or
        compressed
    ¼ cup warm water (lukewarm
        for compressed yeast)
    1 egg
    3½ cups regular all-purpose flour
        (sift before measuring)
    1½ teaspoons salt
    1 teaspoon cardamom
    1 cup seedless raisins
    ⅓ cup chopped citron
    ½ cup slivered blanched almonds

Scald milk. Drop in shortening and sugar, stirring until shortening melts and sugar dissolves. Cool until lukewarm. Dissolve yeast in the warm water; stir into milk. Beat egg slightly and stir into milk mixture. Sift flour again with salt and cardamom. Spoon 2 cups of flour into the liquid and beat until smooth. Mix in raisins, citron, and almonds. Stir in remaining flour until blended.

Place in a greased bowl, cover with a cloth, and set in a warm place until doubled in bulk, 2 to 3 hours. Turn out onto a floured board and knead lightly. Shape into a ball and place on a greased 9-inch layer cake pan. Allow to rise 40 minutes. Bake in a moderate oven (350°) for 45 minutes. Makes 1 round loaf. Cut in ½-inch slices when serving.

VARIATION: The basic bread dough of this recipe can be used in many sweet bread variations. For a handsome coffee bread in an unusual shape, bake balls of sugar-coated dough in a tube pan. Omit cardamom, raisins, citron, and almonds. Cut the dough into pieces the size of a walnut and roll into round balls. Dip the balls in melted butter or margarine and then into a mixture of brown sugar, cinnamon, and chopped nut meats. Place one layer of balls so that they barely touch in a well-greased deep 9-inch tube pan. Sprinkle with raisins. Add another layer of balls and more raisins. Let rise and bake. Turn out of pan and serve hot. The bread breaks easily into serving pieces.

GERMAN BUTTERKUCHEN

Streaks of the rich buttery topping marble this coffee cake.

    1 cup milk
    ½ cup sugar
    1 teaspoon salt
    ¼ cup shortening
    1½ packages yeast, active dry or
        compressed
    1 teaspoon sugar
    ¼ cup warm water (lukewarm
        for compressed yeast)
    2 eggs
    3¼ cups unsifted regular all-purpose
        flour
        Butter topping (recipe follows)
    ⅓ cup chopped almonds

Scald the milk, add the ½ cup sugar, salt, and shortening, and cool to lukewarm. Dissolve the yeast and 1 teaspoon sugar in the warm water, then stir into cooled milk mixture. Beat the eggs with 1 cup of the flour. Add rest of flour alternately with milk-yeast mixture, mixing well after each addition. Pour into a greased 9 by 13-inch baking pan, spreading dough evenly. Set in a warm place to rise for 45 minutes. Sprinkle the butter topping and almonds evenly over top and bake in a moderately hot oven (375°) for 30 minutes, or until lightly browned. Makes 12 squares.

BUTTER TOPPING: Cut ½ cup (¼ lb.) butter into 1 cup sugar and ½ teaspoon cinnamon until fine crumbs develop.

Kügelhopf, studded with fruits and nuts, baked in a fancy mold, is something special to serve with coffee.

KÜGELHOPF

Wonderfully rich and light, Kügelhopf originated in Austria and is now also a French favorite.

>   *1 package yeast, active dry or*
>   *compressed*
>   *¼ cup warm water (lukewarm*
>   *for compressed yeast)*
>   *¾ cup milk, scalded and cooled to*
>   *lukewarm*
>   *¾ cup butter or margarine*
>   *½ cup sugar*
>   *4 eggs, at room temperature*
>   *4 cups regular all-purpose flour*
>   *(sift before measuring)*
>   *1 teaspoon salt*
>   *1 cup golden raisins*
>   *½ cup slivered almonds*
>   *1 tablespoon grated lemon peel*
>   *½ cup finely minced almonds*

In a small bowl dissolve yeast in water, add cooled milk, and stir until blended. In large bowl of your electric mixer, cream butter and sugar until light; add the eggs, one at a time, beating after each addition. Add the yeast mixture and beat until well blended. Sift flour again with salt into mixing bowl. Beat at medium to low speed until batter is smooth. Stir in raisins, almonds, and lemon peel.

Butter a large Kügelhopf mold (or a 10-cup mold) and sprinkle with the minced nuts, turning pan so the bottom and sides will be covered.

For an airy, coarse-textured coffee cake, turn the batter immediately into the buttered mold and let rise as directed below.

For a fine-textured coffee bread, cover bowl lightly and let rise in a warm place until doubled, about 2 hours. Beat batter down and turn into the buttered mold to rise.

Let rise in warm place until batter comes to about ¼ inch of the top of the mold. If you use the traditional Kügelhopf mold or another 10-cup mold with tube, bake in a moderately hot oven (375°) for 50 to 60 minutes. If you use a 10-cup tubeless mold, bake at 350° for 65 to 70 minutes. Bake until cake tester comes out clean. Let cool in pan; turn out. Serves 12.

GERMAN RAISIN BREAD

This sweet yeast dough is potato-moist and fine textured; it is swirled with cinnamon, nuts, and bright candied fruits, and has a surprise of whole blanched almonds placed on bottom of the bread pan to toast during baking. Press rather firmly when you roll the fruits and nuts in the dough, to prevent air spaces from forming as dough rises.

2 packages yeast, active dry or
compressed
1 teaspoon sugar
Warm water (lukewarm for
compressed yeast)
About 8 cups regular all-purpose
flour (sift before measuring)
1 tablespoon salt
2 tablespoons butter or other
shortening
1 cup finely sieved, freshly cooked
potato
2 cups scalded milk, cooled to
lukewarm
2 eggs, slightly beaten
1 cup sugar
¼ cup (⅛ lb.) melted butter
½ teaspoon cinnamon
About 6 tablespoons very soft
butter
½ cup sugar
1½ teaspoons cinnamon
2 cups raisins
2 cups coarsely chopped candied
cherries
1 cup finely chopped nuts
¾ cup chopped citron
Whole blanched almonds
Beaten egg
Butter

Sprinkle or crumble yeast into measuring cup with the 1 teaspoon sugar. Add warm water to make ½ cup; stir to dissolve. Sift 4 cups of the flour again with salt into a large mixing bowl. Add shortening and potato. Stir in milk. Add yeast mixture and mix thoroughly. Cover and allow to rise in a warm place about 2½ hours or until almost doubled.

Beat risen dough slightly. Add eggs, the 1 cup sugar, ¼ cup melted butter, and the ½ teaspoon cinnamon. Gradually add enough more flour (about 4 cups), stirring, to make a soft dough. Turn out on a lightly floured board, and knead until smooth. Place in greased bowl, cover, and allow to rise in a warm place until doubled, about 1 hour. Punch down; divide into 4 parts.

On lightly floured board, roll out each part into a rectangle about 9 by 12 inches. Spread each with an equal amount of the 6 tablespoons butter, and sprinkle with an equal amount of the ½ cup sugar mixed with the 1½ teaspoons cinnamon. Mix together raisins, candied cherries, chopped nuts, and citron. Divide evenly among the 4 portions of dough; spread over the surface of each, leaving about a 1-inch margin on all sides. Roll as you would a jelly roll, starting from a 9-inch side (press firmly but gently as you roll to avoid air spaces). Fold ends under to seal. Place each loaf in a buttered loaf pan (5 by 9 inches) with a few almonds scattered on the bottom. Dip additional almonds in beaten egg and press on top of each loaf to make a pattern.

Cover loaves, and allow to rise in a warm place until almost doubled in bulk, about 1 hour. Bake in a moderate oven (350°) for 45 minutes or until brown. Turn out onto wire rack, then turn upright; brush generously with butter and let cool. Wrap airtight; to freeze loaves, seal in foil. Slice to serve. Makes 4 loaves.

IRISH BARMBRACK

The Irish traditionally serve this sweet bread on Halloween to predict the fortunes of the coming year. Often a ring (to symbolize approaching marriage), a coin (wealth), and a button (many blessings) are put into the loaf.

2 packages yeast, active dry or
    compressed
½ cup warm water (lukewarm
    for compressed yeast)
4 cups regular all-purpose flour
    (sift before measuring)
½ cup sugar
2½ teaspoons salt
1 teaspoon ground allspice
¼ cup (⅛ lb.) softened butter
1 cup scalded milk, cooled
¾ cup seedless raisins
¾ cup currants
½ cup finely chopped candied orange
    or lemon peel
Foil-wrapped ring, coin, or button
    (optional)
2 tablespoons sugar
1 tablespoon water

Dissolve yeast in the ½ cup warm water and set aside for 5 minutes. Sift 2 cups of the flour again with the ½ cup sugar, salt, and allspice. Add the butter and milk to the flour mixture along with the dissolved yeast. Beat the mixture for about 2 minutes with an electric mixer (or 3 to 4 minutes by hand). Cover and set in a warm place until the mixture doubles in volume, about 30 minutes. Then with a wooden spoon, beat in the remaining 2 cups flour, one cup at a time.

Turn dough out onto a well-floured board and knead for about 5 minutes, kneading in the raisins, currants, citrus peel, and foil-wrapped charms, if you wish. Put dough into a clean, greased bowl, turning to grease top of dough. Cover and set in a warm place; let dough rise until doubled in bulk. Then stir down dough, shape into a round, and place on a greased baking sheet. Let rise until almost doubled. Bake in a moderate oven (350°) for about 45 minutes. Mix the 2 tablespoons sugar with the 1 tablespoon water; brush over loaf. Bake for 5 minutes more. Makes 1 loaf.

Raisins, currants, and candied fruits speckle the sweet Irish barmbrack. Serve as is or toasted.

FILLED BUNS

These filled buns are made from a rich sour cream dough that is soft and easy to handle. Shape the buns, then make a deep depression in the center of each bun and fill with thick jam.

¾ cup milk
½ cup (¼ lb.) butter or margarine
1 package yeast, active dry or
    compressed
¼ cup warm water (lukewarm
    for compressed yeast)
5 cups regular all-purpose flour
    (sift before measuring)
½ cup sugar
1½ teaspoons salt
2 egg yolks, slightly beaten
1 cup sour cream
2 egg whites
    About ½ cup jam

Scald the milk, stir in the butter, and cool to lukewarm. Dissolve yeast in the ¼ cup water. Sift flour again with the sugar and salt into a bowl. Add the cooled milk, yeast, egg yolks, and sour cream; stir just until the dough is smooth and blended. Cover and let rise in a warm place about 1½ hours. Stir down dough and turn out on a lightly floured board. Knead gently, adding a little flour as needed, until dough is smooth and elastic. Pinch off pieces and shape into smooth balls, about 1½ inches in diameter. Place on a lightly greased baking sheet, about 2 inches apart, and make a deep depression in the center of each bun with your thumb. Brush each bun with egg white and fill the center with about 1 teaspoon jam. Let the buns rise in a warm place about 40 minutes. Bake in a hot oven (400°) about 10 minutes, or until lightly browned. Serve warm. Makes about 3 dozen buns.

GLAZED LEMON BUNS

These lemon-flavored buns are a great favorite in Chelsea, a riverfront area of London.

    ¼ cup milk
    ½ cup (¼ lb.) butter or margarine
    1 package yeast, active dry or
        compressed
    ¼ cup warm water (lukewarm
        for compressed yeast)
  2¾ cups regular all-purpose flour
        (sift before measuring)
    ½ cup sugar
    ½ teaspoon salt
    1 egg, slightly beaten
        Juice and peel of 1 medium-sized
        lemon
        Lemon glaze (recipe follows)

Scald the milk, stir in the butter, and cool to lukewarm. Dissolve yeast in the ¼ cup water. Sift flour again with the sugar and salt into a bowl. Add the cooled milk, yeast, egg, and lemon juice and peel; beat well. Turn out on a lightly floured board and knead until dough is smooth and elastic. Place dough in a greased bowl, cover, and set in a warm place to rise, about 1½ hours. Stir down dough, pinch off pieces, and shape into smooth, rounded buns about 1½ inches in diameter.

Place buns on a greased baking sheet about 2 inches apart; let rise in a warm place until doubled in bulk, about 30 minutes. Bake in a hot oven (400°) for 10 to 12 minutes or until lightly

browned; cool on racks about 5 minutes before glazing. Then drizzle the top of each bun with about 1 tablespoon glaze. Serve warm. Makes 1½ dozen buns.

LEMON GLAZE: Blend together 1 cup sifted powdered sugar, 2 teaspoons lemon juice, and 2 teaspoons water; beat until smooth.

MEXICAN PAN DULCE

The Mexicans often serve these round, flat sweet buns with morning coffee. They call them *pan dulce*, which means simply sweet bread.

    1 package yeast, active dry or
        compressed
    ¾ cup warm water (lukewarm
        for compressed yeast)
  3½ cups regular all-purpose flour
        (sift before measuring)
    ¾ cup sugar
    ½ teaspoon salt
    3 tablespoons melted butter or
        margarine
    2 eggs, slightly beaten
        Cinnamon-flavored topping
        (recipe follows)

Dissolve the yeast in the ¾ cup water. Sift flour again with the sugar and salt into a bowl. Add the yeast, butter, and eggs; beat until smooth. Place dough in a greased bowl, cover, and let rise in a warm place until doubled in bulk, about 1½ hours.

Stir down, turn out onto a lightly floured board, and knead until smooth and elastic. Pinch off pieces of dough and shape into smooth, rounded balls about 1¼ inches in diameter. Place balls of dough on a greased baking sheet, about 2 inches apart. With the palm of your hand, press each ball down, flattening it slightly. Gently spread about 1 tablespoon topping on each bun, and then let buns rise until doubled in bulk, about 30 minutes. Bake in a hot oven (400°) for 10 minutes, or until lightly browned. Serve warm. Makes about 18

CINNAMON-FLAVORED TOPPING: Blend together 1 cup sugar, 1 cup sifted flour, ½ cup (¼ lb.) melted butter or margarine, 1 slightly beaten egg, 1 teaspoon cinnamon, and a dash of salt.

DANISH PASTRY

Danish pastry (it is known in Denmark as *Wienerbrod*, or Vienna bread) is not difficult to make if you follow precisely the directions we give here. If we were to stress only one point, it would be that you should keep the dough as cold as possible so that it will not be sticky while you work with it. Our directions call for chilling the dough at least five times; however, if your kitchen is especially warm, you may need to chill it even more.

Make the fillings you want to use before you make the dough, so they will be cool when you use them. You can make them the day before and store them in the refrigerator. Each filling recipe makes about 1 cup, and the fillings can be used almost interchangeably to fill the pastries. You can make the pastry and keep the unbaked dough in the refrigerator overnight before shaping.

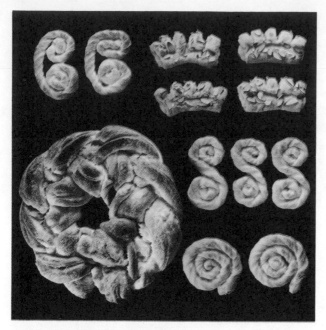

You can make buttery, flaky Danish pastry in any of these shapes. Pictured above (clockwise from top left) are pretzel-shaped twists, cockscomb, S and snail-shaped twists, and large wreath.

1½ cups soft butter or margarine
4½ cups regular all-purpose flour
       (sift before measuring)
  2 packages yeast, active dry or compressed
  ¼ cup warm water (lukewarm
       for compressed yeast)
  1 cup cold milk, unscalded
  1 egg, slightly beaten
  3 tablespoons sugar
  ½ teaspoon ground cardamom (optional)
  ½ teaspoon salt

Cream butter with ½ cup of the flour until well blended, and chill for 30 to 45 minutes. Soften yeast in warm water; add milk, egg, sugar, cardamom, and salt. Stir in 2 cups of flour. Beat with spoon until dough is smooth and elastic; beat in remaining flour until well blended. Turn out on lightly floured board, form into ball, dust with flour, roll into a 16-inch square.

Turn butter-flour mixture out on floured board; roll and shape into a rectangle 8 by 16 inches (it should roll out like pie crust; if too soft, chill longer). Place on one half of the yeast dough. Turn other half of dough over butter to encase it. Pinch edges together to seal. With a rolling pin, lightly pound dough to about 12 by 16 inches. Fold ⅓ of dough over center, then fold remaining ⅓ over center. Chill in refrigerator for 30 minutes, or in freezer for 10 minutes (don't freeze it).

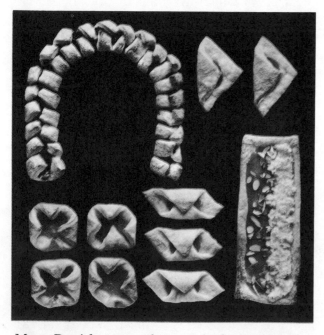

More Danish pastry shapes (clockwise from top left): prune wreath, envelope tarts, Danish pastry strip, sheath tarts, and packet tarts. All but the twists in top photograph have fillings.

Pound dough lightly again into a rectangle, then roll into a 16-inch square and fold side thirds over center again; chill. Repeat pounding, rolling, folding, and chilling three times more. After final chilling, shape, fill, and decorate.

Place shaped pastries on lightly greased baking sheets. Chill for about 45 minutes. Bake in moderately hot oven (375°) for 25 minutes (unless otherwise directed), or until golden brown. Makes about 36 pastries.

APRICOT OR PRUNE FILLING:

1 cup dried apricots or pitted prunes
1 cup water
½ cup sugar

Simmer apricots or prunes in the water until tender, about 20 minutes. Add sugar. Force through a strainer or whirl in a blender until smooth.

ALMOND FILLING:

1 can (8 oz.) almond paste
1 cup sifted powdered sugar
1 egg

Mix together almond paste, powdered sugar, and egg until well blended.

COCONUT LEMON FILLING OR TOPPING:

1 cup packaged grated coconut
2 tablespoons lemon juice
½ cup sifted powdered sugar

In a small bowl, blend together coconut, lemon juice, and powdered sugar.

VANILLA CUSTARD:

1 cup light cream
1 tablespoon flour
2 egg yolks
2 tablespoons sugar
2 teaspoons vanilla

In a small saucepan, combine cream, flour, egg yolks, and sugar. Cook over low heat, stirring occasionally, until thickened and smooth. Add vanilla. Cool.

BUTTER CREAM:

½ cup (¼ lb.) butter
1 cup sifted powdered sugar

Cream together butter and powdered sugar until smooth.

TARTS (Wienerbrod Taerte)

Make 1 recipe Danish Pastry. Roll pastry out on a lightly floured board into a 24-inch square. Cut in 6 strips, each 4 inches wide. Cut each pastry strip into 4-inch squares. Place about 1 teaspoon of any filling in center of each square. You can fold these to make three differently shaped tarts: envelope *(Konvolut)*—fold one corner to point about 1 inch from opposite corner; sheath *(Skede)*—fold two opposite corners to overlap ½ inch in center; packet *(Pakke)*—fold all four corners to center, overlapping slightly. Brush with water and sprinkle with sugar. Each pastry strip makes 6.

DANISH PASTRY STRIP

Make 1 recipe Danish Pastry. Roll pastry out on a lightly floured board into a 24-inch square. Cut in 6 strips, each 4 inches wide. Have ready your choice of fruit or nut filling. Roll up edges of each pastry strip, pinching corners to make a stand-up ridge. Spread about ½ cup filling in a 2-inch-wide band down center of pastry strip to within 1 inch of ends. Top with 1-inch band of Vanilla Custard or Coconut Lemon Filling. Sprinkle with sugar and sliced almonds. Each strip serves 3 to 4.

CINNAMON CAKE (Rolade)

Roll out one recipe of Danish Pastry into a 24-inch square. Cut a 6-inch strip of the pastry, fold in thirds, and roll out to fit the bottom of a pan about 10 by 15 inches.

Lightly butter pan and fit in the pastry. Spread remaining pastry with ½ cup Butter Cream and sprinkle with cinnamon sugar (¼ cup sugar, 2 teaspoons cinnamon). Roll up as for a jelly roll, and cut 1-inch-wide slices from roll.

To fold and roll pastry: Place butter mixture on half of dough; fold, seal. Use rolling pin to pound dough to rectangle. Fold top third over center, then bottom third over center.

Filled tart starts with square of pastry, can be folded any of three different ways after placing filling in center. Cockscomb is 4-inch strip filled, folded lengthwise, cut as shown.

Arrange slices, cut side down, evenly on pastry-lined pan. Lightly roll across top to flatten slices so they almost touch each other. Sprinkle top of cake with ½ cup sliced almonds. Chill 30 minutes and bake in a moderately hot oven (375°) for 45 minutes or until golden brown. Cut in squares to serve. Makes 15 servings.

WREATH (Krans)

Make 1 recipe Danish Pastry. Roll pastry out on a lightly floured board into a 24-inch square. Cut in 6 strips, each 4 inches wide. Use three strips of the pastry for one wreath and about 1½ cups of any of the fillings. Spread about ½ cup filling in a 1-inch band down center of each strip. Fold long

sides of each over center to encase the filling, brush with water, press lightly to seal. Braid the three strands together, keeping seams up. Form the braid into a wreath; pinch ends together lightly. Brush with water and sprinkle with sugar. Each wreath serves 10 to 12.

PRUNE WREATH
(Sveske Krans)

Make 1 recipe Danish Pastry. Roll pastry out on a lightly floured board into a 24-inch square. Cut in 6 strips, each 4 inches wide. Spread ¼ cup Butter Cream in a 1-inch band down center of a pastry strip. Spoon about 1 cup Prune Filling down center

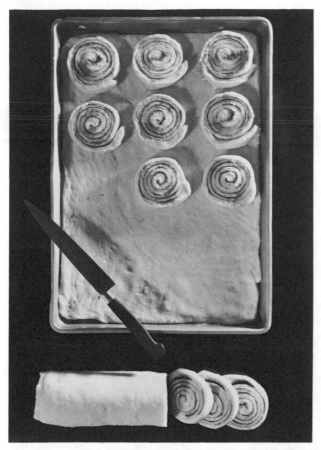

For Cinnamon Cake (page 51) you cover bottom of pan with a thin sheet of dough; spread remaining dough with sugar-cinnamon mixture, roll up, slice, arrange on dough in pan.

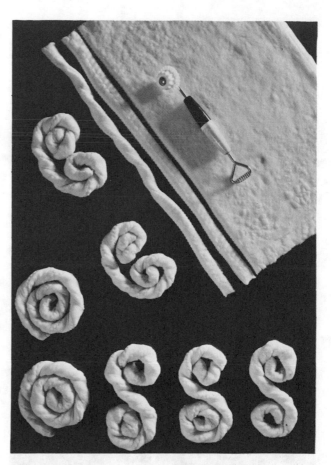

Three shapes to make from ½-inch-wide pastry strips. You first twist the pastry strip lengthwise, then turn ends of twisted strip to make pretzel, snail, or S-shaped pastries.

of Butter Cream. Make slashes toward center about 1½ inches deep and 1 inch apart on long sides of pastry. Fold cut pieces over filling, alternating right and left sides. Form into a wreath or horseshoe shape. Brush with water and sprinkle with sugar. Each wreath serves 6 to 8.

PASTRY TWISTS

Roll 1 recipe of Danish Pastry out on a lightly floured board into an 18-inch square. Cut into 36 strips, each about ½ inch wide. Twist strands lengthwise so they look like a rope. Curl twisted strand into a spiral to form Snail, or curl twisted strand on both ends to shape a large S. After shaping, brush with water and sprinkle with sugar.

COCKSCOMB (Hanekam)

Make 1 recipe Danish Pastry. Roll pastry out on a lightly floured board into a 24-inch square. Cut in 6 strips, each 4 inches wide. Spread about ½ cup Butter Cream in a 1½-inch-wide band down center of a pastry strip. Spoon ½ cup Almond Filling down center of Butter Cream. Fold long sides to center, overlapping about ½ inch; brush edges with water and seal. Sprinkle board next to strip with sugar and sliced almonds, brush pastry with water, and turn over onto almonds and sugar; repeat to coat both sides with sugar and almonds. Roll lightly with rolling pin. Cut into 6 pieces, 4 inches wide. On each piece, cut 4 slashes 1 inch deep from one folded edge to center; turn slightly to separate slashes. Each strip makes 6.

Finnish Easter Bread is baked in a pail. Let dough rise in pail until doubled, then put in oven and bake for about 1½ hours.

Mammoth loaf is ready to serve. Cut loaf into quarters, then cut each quarter in crosswise slices. Serve with butter and cheese.

FINNISH EASTER BREAD

This mushroom-shaped Easter bread, called *Pääsiäisleipä* in Finnish, is rich with butter and milk and the pungent flavors of citrus and cardamom. Traditionally, *Pääsiäisleipä* is baked in a milking pail to celebrate the birth of spring calves and the abundance of dairy foods.

To serve the bread, cut the whole loaf into quarters, then slice each quarter to make triangular slices. It's delicious with soft cheeses such as Camembert, Brie, breakfast cheese, or natural cream cheese. And hard cheeses such as Edam, Swiss, or smoked Gouda are also excellent accompaniments.

      2 packages yeast, active dry or
            compressed
   ½ cup warm water (lukewarm
            for compressed yeast)
1 ½ cups light cream, scalded and
            cooled (or undiluted
            evaporated milk)
      2 cups unsifted regular all-purpose
            flour
      5 egg yolks
      1 cup sugar
      1 cup (½ lb.) melted and cooled
            butter
1 ½ teaspoons salt
      2 teaspoons fresh ground cardamom
      2 teaspoons fresh grated lemon peel
      2 tablespoons grated orange peel
      1 cup golden raisins
      1 cup chopped blanched almonds
      1 cup milk, scalded and cooled
      2 cups rye flour
      4 to 4½ cups unsifted regular
            all-purpose flour

Dissolve yeast in the water in a large bowl. Stir in the cream and 2 cups regular all-purpose flour, and beat until smooth. Cover, and let rise in a warm place until doubled in size, ½ to 1 hour. Stir in the egg yolks, sugar, butter, salt, cardamom, lemon peel, orange peel, raisins, and almonds, and beat well until thoroughly combined. Stir in the one cup milk and the rye flour until combined, then stir in all but ½ cup of the remaining regular all-purpose flour to make a stiff dough. Sprinkle last ½ cup flour on board; turn dough out onto floured board and knead until smooth, about 10 minutes. Butter the bowl and place kneaded dough into it; turn dough over to grease top, cover lightly, and let rise until dough is doubled in size.

Punch dough down, and work into a smooth ball. Place dough, rounded side up, in a well buttered (straight sided) 4-quart pail (do not use a galvanized pail) and let rise until dough is almost doubled in bulk and just comes to the top of the pail. Or divide into two 2-quart-sized sand pails or two 2-pound coffee cans. Bake in a moderate oven (350°) for about 1½ hours for a 4-quart pail, or 1 hour for a 2-quart pail. Before removing from oven, test with long straw or wooden skewer. Brush top of loaf with butter while hot, and let cool in the pail for about 20 minutes before turning out. Cut loaf in quarters and slice; makes about 40 slices.

PORTUGUESE SWEET BREAD

This very fine-textured, golden Easter bread from the Azore Islands is made in traditionally shaped round loaves, with a hard-cooked egg baked in the center of each and a symbolic cross of the bread on top. Each small loaf is an individual serving. The same rich dough, when used on other holidays, is simply shaped into plain rolls.

*2 packages yeast, active dry or
    compressed
¼ cup warm water (lukewarm
    for compressed yeast)
1 cup sugar
1 cup milk, scalded and still hot
¼ cup (⅛ lb.) butter
1 teaspoon salt
3 eggs, well beaten
6 to 7 cups regular all-purpose flour
    (sift before measuring)
6 cold hard-cooked eggs
    (omit if making rolls)*

Dissolve yeast in warm water. In a large bowl, mix together sugar, hot milk, butter, and salt; stir until butter melts. When cooled to lukewarm, beat in eggs and yeast mixture. Gradually beat 5 cups

of the flour into liquid, blending until smooth.

Flour a board heavily with part of the remaining flour. Turn soft dough out onto board, and sprinkle dough with more flour. Knead until very smooth and small air-filled blisters form on surface of dough (about 15 to 20 minutes), adding flour to board as needed. Place dough in a large buttered bowl. Keep covered in a warm place and let rise until doubled in bulk, about 2 hours. Punch down dough. Butter hands to work with dough. This amount of dough will make 6 small individual-size loaves or 2 pans (9-inch-square size) of rolls.

To make loaves, make a ball of dough about 2½ inches in diameter. Pinch off about ¼ of the ball of dough and set aside. Shape larger portion into a flat round cake about ½ inch thick. Place on a greased baking sheet and gently press a hard-cooked egg into the center of the dough. Form the small portion of dough into 2 round strips about 6 inches long. Cross in an X over the egg and pinch ends to underside of loaf. Make a collar of double thickness foil about 6 inches in diameter and ¾ inch high. Set around the loaf. Allow 1 inch between rings on the baking sheet.

To shape rolls, make smooth balls of dough about 1 inch in diameter and place about ⅛ inch apart in a greased 9-inch-square pan.

Cover shaped dough lightly and set in a warm place to rise again, for about 1 hour or until almost doubled in size. Bake in a moderate oven (350°) for 20 minutes, or until golden brown. Serve hot, or cool (out of pans) on wire racks and wrap airtight (the bread freezes well). To reheat, place cool or thawed bread in a paper bag, sprinkle bag with water and put in a hot oven (400°) for about 10 minutes. Serve with sweet butter and fruit jam or jelly.

HOT CROSS BUNS

Breads and buns seem to have been decorated with crosses even in ancient Babylonia and Egypt. But the familiar small hot cross buns date back to England of the 1300's, when they were served on Good Friday and allegedly given to far-traveling churchgoers on Easter Sunday.

1 cup milk
2 tablespoons butter or margarine
1 package yeast, active dry or
*   compressed*
¼ cup warm water (lukewarm
*   for compressed yeast)*
4 cups regular all-purpose flour
*   (sift before measuring)*
⅓ cup sugar
¾ teaspoon salt
¾ teaspoon cinnamon
¼ teaspoon cloves
¼ teaspoon nutmeg
¾ cup currants
¼ cup finely diced candied orange
*   peel or citron*
2 eggs, well beaten
1 egg yolk diluted with 1 teaspoon
*   water for topping*
Lemon frosting (recipe follows)

Scald the milk, stir in the butter, and cool to lukewarm. Dissolve yeast in the ¼ cup warm water. Sift flour again with the sugar, salt, cinnamon, cloves, and nutmeg. Combine the flour mixture with currants and orange peel; stir in the eggs, cooled milk, and yeast; blend well. Turn dough out onto a lightly floured board and knead until smooth and elastic. Place in a greased bowl, cover, and let rise in a warm place until doubled in bulk, about 1½ hours.

Stir down dough, pinch off pieces, and form smooth, rounded balls about 1¼ inches in diameter. Place balls of dough on a lightly greased baking sheet about 2 inches apart. Brush each bun lightly with the egg yolk and water topping. Let the buns rise in a warm place until doubled in bulk, about 30 minutes. Bake in a hot oven (400°) for about 10 minutes, or until lightly browned. Cool on racks about 5 minutes. Then, with a spoon or the tip of a knife, drizzle frosting on top of each bun to form a small cross. Serve warm. Makes 3 dozen buns.

If you freeze these buns, let them cool thoroughly without frosting; wrap tightly. Heat the frozen buns on a baking sheet in a hot oven (400°) for about 3 to 5 minutes. Then cool and decorate.

LEMON FROSTING: Combine 1 cup sifted powdered sugar, 2 teaspoons lemon juice, and 1 teaspoon water; beat until smooth.

ANISE KUCHEN

Grated lemon and orange peels tone down the spicy anise flavor in this German bread which is particularly good when toasted. To crush the anise seed, either grind it with a mortar and pestle or roll it on a bread board.

1¼ cups milk
1 package yeast, active dry or
*   compressed*
¼ cup warm water (lukewarm
*   for compressed yeast)*
1 cup (½ lb.) butter or margarine
½ cup sugar
Grated peel of 1 lemon
Grated peel of ½ orange
1 teaspoon salt
¼ teaspoon mace
¼ teaspoon nutmeg
3 tablespoons anise seed, ground
*   or crushed*
3 eggs
About 4 cups regular all-purpose
*   flour (sift before measuring)*

Scald milk and cool to lukewarm. Dissolve yeast in the warm water. Cream butter and gradually add sugar, creaming until light and fluffy. Mix in the grated lemon and orange peels, salt, mace, nutmeg, and crushed anise seed. Add the eggs, one at a time, beating well after each addition. Stir in the dissolved yeast and the milk. Gradually beat in flour, adding enough more flour to make a soft dough. Turn out on a lightly floured board, cover dough, and let rest for 10 minutes.

A gay ribbon-tied "package" of this spicy Anise Kuchen is a thoughtful gift to give at Christmas time.

Knead until smooth and elastic, using as little additional flour as possible. Place dough in a large greased bowl, cover, and set in a warm place to rise. When nearly doubled in bulk, punch down and turn out on a lightly floured board. Divide dough in half and shape into two 5 by 8-inch loaves. Place on a 12 by 18-inch greased baking sheet, allowing several inches between loaves. Grease the top of dough lightly with a thin coating of melted shortening or salad oil. Tie each loaf with heavy brown paper strips, cut 1½ inches wide, to make depressions for ribbon.

Let dough rise in a warm place until almost doubled in bulk. Bake in a moderate oven (350°) for 45 minutes or until golden brown. When cool, remove the paper strips and replace with a bright ribbon 1½ inches wide. Makes 2 loaves.

EASTER PIGEONS

These pigeons shaped from sweet yeast dough add a festive look to the Easter breakfast table. The recipe makes two large pigeons or 12 small ones.

1¾ cups milk
  1 package yeast, active dry or
      compressed
¼ cup warm water (lukewarm
      for compressed yeast)
⅓ cup sugar
  2 teaspoons salt
  2 eggs, beaten
  3 to 4 cups regular all-purpose flour
      (sift before measuring)
½ cup (¼ lb.) melted butter or
      margarine

SWEET YEAST BREADS 57

Sweet yeast dough is shaped into large and small pigeons for an Easter breakfast treat.

Scald milk and cool to lukewarm. Dissolve yeast in the warm water and add to the lukewarm milk. Add sugar and salt. Stir in beaten eggs. Gradually add 2 cups of the flour, beating until smooth. Add melted butter and mix well. Add enough more flour to make a soft dough. Turn out on a lightly floured board and knead lightly. Cover with a cloth and let rest 15 minutes. Knead again until smooth and elastic. Put in a greased bowl, cover, let rise in a warm place until almost double in bulk, about 1 hour.

Punch down dough and roll out on a lightly floured board to a ½-inch thickness.

Cut the dough into strips 1 inch wide, and roll each strip into a rope ½ inch thick. Cut the ropes into 9-inch lengths. Tie each dough rope in a loose knot, leaving one end short. Put on greased baking sheet. Pinch the short end to shape a head and beak; poke a clove in the head for an eye. Flatten the other end for the tail; snip end of tail twice. Let rise. Brush with slightly beaten egg. Bake in a hot oven (400°) for 15 minutes.

To make the large pigeons, cut dough into 2-inch-wide strips; roll into ropes 1 inch thick, and cut each rope into 12-inch lengths. Shape pigeons as described above; bake in a hot oven (400°) for 20 minutes.

CHRISTMAS TREE BREAD

You'll probably discover that it is easier than you expect to shape this fancy looking bread. One package of hot roll mix makes two Christmas trees.

> 1 package (14 oz.) hot roll mix
> ¾ cup warm water
> 1 egg, beaten
> 1 tablespoon sugar
> ½ teaspoon salt
> ½ teaspoon ground nutmeg or
>   cinnamon, or anise flavoring
> ¼ cup (⅛ lb.) soft butter
>   Fruit filling
>   Powdered sugar icing
>   Candied cherries and citron
>   (optional)

FRUIT FILLING:
1½ cups cut-up cooked dried figs,
     apricots, or prunes (or a
     combination of dried fruits)
½ teaspoon nutmeg
½ teaspoon cinnamon
 1 teaspoon grated lemon peel
 1 tablespoon lemon juice
¼ cup sugar

Soften the yeast packet from package of mix in the warm water. Combine yeast with egg, sugar, salt, and flavoring. Gradually add flour from mix, beating well between each addition. Dough should be smooth. Grease top of dough and let rise in a warm place until nearly doubled in bulk. Turn out on lightly floured board and knead gently, then divide in half. Roll each piece of dough into a rectangle about 14 by 4 inches. Cover and let dough rest for about 20 minutes. Meanwhile, combine ingredients for filling.

Working with one rectangle of dough at a time, spread each with half of the butter, then cover with half of the filling. Starting from a long side, roll up like a jelly roll; taper each end. Place on a greased cooky sheet. Using scissors, clip down one side, clipping to within ¼ inch of the opposite side—clips should be ½ inch apart. Separate the clipped slices by pulling one to the left and the next to the right. As you work turn each slice to show the filling—this forms the branches.

Here are decorative ways to present Christmas breads: Pineapple Butterscotch Whirl is baked and served in round griddle, the edge outlined by candles in old-fashioned clip-on holders. Honey-Filbert Crescents (page 60) are on platter edged with greens, shiny balls. Tiny Swedish candle holders accent tree branches.

Cover and let rise until almost doubled. Bake in a moderately hot oven (375°) for 15 to 20 minutes. Cool, then spoon on frosting made by mixing a small amount of water with powdered sugar until paste consistency—outline branches of tree with the frosting. Decorate with candied cherries and bits of citron, if you wish. Makes 2 trees.

PINEAPPLE BUTTERSCOTCH WHIRL

To shape this unusual bread whirl, you coil long ropes of dough onto a round griddle or pizza pan. Crushed pineapple in a butterscotch syrup glazes the top.

1 package yeast, active dry or
    compressed
2 tablespoons warm water (lukewarm
    for compressed yeast)
½ cup milk
3 tablespoons shortening
¼ cup sugar
1 teaspoon salt
2½ cups regular all-purpose flour
    (sift before measuring)
1 egg, beaten
    Pineapple Topping (recipe follows)

Dissolve yeast in warm water. Scald milk; add shortening, sugar, and salt; cool to lukewarm. Sift flour again and add to milk along with egg and dissolved yeast; mix to a moderately stiff dough. Turn out on lightly floured board, and knead gently until smooth. Place in a greased bowl and let rise until nearly doubled, about 1½ hours.

Divide dough into 6 equal parts. Roll each piece of dough with your hands until it forms a rope about 18 inches long. Beginning at the outer edge of a greased round pizza pan or round griddle about 12 inches in diameter, coil the ropes around, gradually working in toward the center. Pinch the ends of the pieces of dough together to make one continuous whirl that ends in the center of the pan.

Flatten the whirl with your fingers until the pan surface is evenly covered with dough. Spread Pineapple Topping over whirl to within ½ inch of the outer edge. Let rise until nearly doubled, 40 to 45 minutes. Bake in a moderately hot oven (375°) for 30 to 45 minutes. Serves 8 to 10.

PINEAPPLE TOPPING: Blend together ¼ cup (⅛ lb.) soft butter or margarine, ¾ cup brown sugar, and 1 can (9 oz.) crushed pineapple, well drained.

HONEY-FILBERT CRESCENTS

A honey and nut topping is spread over each of these crescent buns before you remove them from the oven.

> 1 package yeast, active dry or
>   compressed
> 2 tablespoons warm water (lukewarm
>   for compressed yeast)
> 6 tablespoons milk
> 3 tablespoons shortening
> ¼ cup sugar
> 1 teaspoon salt
> 1 egg, beaten
> 2¼ cups regular all-purpose flour
>   (sift before measuring)
> 2 tablespoons soft butter or
>   margarine
> ¼ cup sugar
> 1 teaspoon cinnamon
>   Melted butter
>   Honey-Filbert Topping
>   (recipe follows)

Dissolve yeast in the warm water; scald milk; add shortening, sugar, and salt; stir until blended;

cool to lukewarm. Add egg and yeast; stir vigorously. Add flour and beat to a moderately stiff dough. Knead gently on a lightly floured board a few seconds, just to smooth out dough.

Put dough back into bowl, cover, and let rise until nearly doubled in bulk, about 1 hour. Turn out on floured board and divide in half. Roll each piece into a circle about 8 inches in diameter. Cover each circle with half of the soft butter; sprinkle each with half of a mixture of the sugar and cinnamon.

With a sharp knife, cut each circle into 8 equal pie-shaped pieces. Starting from outer edge, roll up each triangle to its point. Arrange rolls with point side down on buttered pan (about 11 by 7 inches), so that the rolls just touch each other. Curve pointed ends to make crescent shapes. Cover and let rise until nearly doubled, about 50 minutes.

Brush tops with melted butter and place in a hot oven (400°). After 10 minutes baking, remove pan and immediately spread with warm Honey-Filbert Topping. Return crescents to oven and continue baking 10 to 15 minutes, or until done. Let stand in pan a few minutes before turning out. Makes 16 crescents.

HONEY-FILBERT TOPPING: Combine ¼ cup honey, ⅓ cup sugar, 3 tablespoons butter, ⅛ teaspoon cinnamon, ¼ cup chopped filberts. Heat until mixture just begins to boil; remove and cool slightly. (Mixture may be reheated if it becomes too firm on cooling.)

CHRISTOPSOMO
(Greek Christmas Bread)

Identified by a symbolic cross on top, Christopsomo is a large golden Greek yeast loaf rich with eggs. It is excellent served warm, the anise-scented slices spread with sweet or regular butter; and it's equally as good later when toasted and served with honey.

2 packages yeast, active dry or
    compressed
½ cup warm water (lukewarm for
    compressed yeast)
½ cup milk, scalded and cooled
1 cup (½ lb.) butter or margarine,
    melted and cooled to lukewarm
4 eggs, slightly beaten
¾ cup sugar
2 teaspoons crushed anise seed
1 teaspoon salt
7 cups unsifted regular all-purpose
    flour
9 candied cherries or walnut halves
1 egg white, slightly beaten

Blend yeast with warm water and let stand until softened, about 5 minutes. Combine in a large bowl the yeast mixture, milk, butter, eggs, sugar, anise seed, and salt; blend thoroughly. Gradually beat in the flour.

Turn dough onto a lightly floured board and knead for 10 minutes or until dough is smooth and elastic. Place in a large greased bowl (the one in which you mixed the bread dough), turning so surface is coated with the fat. Cover and let rise in a warm place for about 2 hours or until almost doubled in size.

Punch dough down and pinch off two pieces, each 3 inches in diameter, and set aside. Knead remaining dough on unfloured board to make a smooth ball. Place on a greased baking sheet and flatten into a 9 to 10-inch round.

Shape each of the 3-inch balls into a 15-inch-long rope by rolling on an unfloured board under the palm of your hand. Cut a 5-inch-long slash into each end of the two ropes. Cross ropes on the center of the round loaf; *do not press down.* Curl slashed sections away from center of each rope (see photograph). Place a candied cherry or walnut

Lightly arrange two ropes of dough on Greek Christmas loaf; curl slashed ends inward.

Dough strips atop baked loaf resemble one form of Christian cross. Bread is mildly sweet.

half in each curl and one in the center of the cross. Brush the loaf with the beaten egg white. Cover loaf lightly and set in a warm place. Let rise for about 1 hour or until almost doubled in size.

Bake in a moderate oven (350°) for 45 minutes or until a thin wooden skewer inserted in center of loaf comes out clean. Serve hot, or let cool on wire rack. Cut in wedges or slices. To reheat, wrap bread in foil and place in a moderate oven (350°) for 40 minutes. Makes 1 large loaf.

SOURDOUGH BREADS

In the old West, when they said "sourdough" they literally meant *sour dough*. The zesty sour aroma floated from starter crocks everywhere—from chuck wagon larders, homesteaders' kitchens, covered wagons, and miners' tents.

To the pioneers, the "starter" gained its ability to leaven and impart its characteristic tangy flavor and texture from some mysterious unknown force. Old starters were carefully guarded and shared with family and friends. Woodsmen and hunters would walk several miles to get a starter from someone who was known to have a particularly good strain. Some strains were said to be more than 30 years old—and of superior quality because of age. Now after much fiction, folklore, and practical use of sourdough in many bread products, food technologists are beginning to study the scientific aspects of the phenomenon of sourdough. In research in our test kitchens on how starters could be made, we uncovered a method of making a sourdough starter that was handed down from a Northern California cattleman. We tried it. It worked. We tried again under slightly different conditions and had no luck. After repeated tries (many successful, some not), we realized that you can't be sure of achieving every time a successful growth of the particular microorganism that gives sourdough its flavor and leavening.

Variety of sourdough breads: (left to right), date loaf, bread sticks, corn French bread, dinner rolls, holiday braid, corn sticks.

SOURDOUGH STARTER

The authentic sourdough of the early pioneers in the West and Alaska is a simple combination of milk and flour that is kept in a warm place until it begins to bubble from the activity of a special bacterial fermentation. The organisms that are responsible for this fermentation are present in milk. If you are unsuccessful in your first attempt to make a starter, it may be because the necessary bacteria were not present in the milk you used or because the temperature was not high enough to sustain the fermentation action. Try again with milk from a different dairy.

To make the starter, place 1 cup milk in a glass jar or crock (nothing metal) and allow to stand at room temperature for 24 hours. Stir in 1 cup flour. Leave uncovered in a warm place (80° is ideal) for two to five days, depending on how long it takes to bubble and sour. A good place is near the pilot light on a gas range; do not place it too close to the pilot light, however, because too much heat will stop the fermentation. If it starts to dry out, stir in enough tepid water to bring it back to the original consistency. Once it has a good sour aroma and is full of bubbles it is ready to use.

Try to maintain about 1½ cups starter.

Each time you use part of your starter, replenish it with a mixture of equal amounts of milk and flour. Leave at room temperature several hours or overnight or until it again becomes full of bubbles, then cover and store it in the refrigerator.

The starter is best if you use it at least once a week. If you do not use it for two or three weeks,

Spongy texture of this starter indicates that yeast cells are present and ready for use.

spoon out and discard about half of the starter and replenish it as described above. Given good care a starter becomes more flavorful with age. If you don't plan to use the starter for several weeks, it is a good idea to freeze it. Since this will slow down the yeast action, you should leave it at room temperature for 24 hours after thawing.

You can also purchase dehydrated commercial starters at many specialty food stores and gift shops. Use and keep the commercial starter as we described above. Once you have your starter and work with it a while, you'll get to know it as an old friend. You'll know how to control the sourness to suit your own taste, and how long it will take to act (rise) in the products you make throughout the year. (It works faster in warmer months.)

With an active starter, you are ready to try some of the following recipes. There are a few variables that you learn to understand as you work with sourdough. A double leavening action exists in all of these recipes: from the reaction of acid (directly related to the sourness) with soda; and from the yeast action in the starter. The more sour your starter, the more soda you must add. Begin by using the suggested amount, which is based on average sourness. With experience you can judge the proper amount—don't increase or decrease it

more than 50 per cent. You will also find that the proofing (rising) times will vary with temperature —the cooler it is, the longer you allow.

CAMP COOKERY WITH SOURDOUGH

Sourdough is well-suited to outdoor and camp cooking. Biscuits, cookies, and corn bread are all candidates for the reflector oven. Use the same baking times as for regular ovens (or slightly less) and control the browning by moving the reflector oven closer to or farther from the fire. The flour measurements are for unsifted flour—that's what the pioneers used, and besides you don't want to take a sifter camping.

When you're camping, it's good to use the starter daily and replenish it with fresh or undiluted evaporated milk and flour as you do at home. Daytime temperatures should keep it growing. If you don't use it daily, store it in an ice chest, or discard half and replace the loss with milk and flour (as described previously on this page).

To make biscuits or pancakes for breakfast, start the initial "sponge" the night before; cover the crock containing it and place it in a warm place to rise—near the coals of the campfire, for example. If the nights are exceptionally cold, you will have to start your products earlier in the afternoon to have them rise by morning.

SOURDOUGH FRENCH BREAD

Anyone who has visited San Francisco will recall the hard-crusted, tangy loaves of sourdough bread made by that city's French and Italian bakers. It is not possible to give here a recipe that will produce that exact same bread—because the character of those loaves comes from the special ovens, the particular starter strain, and controls and equipment that cannot be duplicated in the home. But we have developed sourdough French-type breads with good sour flavor and fragrance, dark crusts, and chewy texture. There are two methods of preparation; the bread made by the short method has commercial yeast and is lighter and less sour than long-method bread.

Hard wheat flour gives the best textured bread, but if you cannot easily obtain it, regular all-purpose flour works most acceptably.

This recipe makes two oblong loaves or one large round loaf. The crust should be darker than that of regular white bread.

SHORT METHOD

1½ cups warm water (lukewarm for
compressed yeast)
1 package yeast, active dry or
compressed
1 cup starter
4 cups unsifted regular all-purpose
flour
2 teaspoons sugar
2 teaspoons salt
About ½ teaspoon soda
About 2 cups unsifted regular
all-purpose flour

Pour warm water into a large mixing bowl; stir in the yeast. Add starter, the 4 cups flour, salt, and sugar. Stir vigorously for about 3 minutes with a wooden spoon. Turn into a large greased bowl, cover with a towel and let rise in a warm place until doubled in bulk (1½ to 2 hours). Mix soda with 1 cup of the remaining flour and stir in; the dough will be very stiff. Turn dough out onto a floured board and begin kneading; add the remaining 1 cup flour (or more) to control the stickiness. Knead until satiny—at least 8 minutes, until the dough cannot absorb any more flour.

Shape into two oblong loaves or one large round loaf. Place on a *lightly* greased cooky sheet, cover, and place in a warm place; let rise until nearly doubled in size—1 to 1½ hours. Just before baking, brush outside with water; make diagonal slashes across the top with a sharp knife or a single-edge razor. Put a shallow pan of hot water in the bottom of oven. (If you prefer a more tender crust, do not place the pan of water in the oven, and brush the unbaked loaf with salad oil or butter instead of water.) Bake in a hot oven (400°) until the crust is medium dark brown (about 45 minutes for oblong loaves and about 50 minutes for the

large round loaf). For a heavier and tougher crust, remove loaf from oven 10 minutes before it is done; brush with salted water and return to a very hot oven (425°) to bake for the remaining time.

LONG METHOD

Plan on 24 hours from start to finish for this sourdough bread. The longer time allows more sourness and wild yeast action to develop. It is more dense in texture than the loaf made with commercial yeast.

1½ cups warm water
1 cup starter
4 cups unsifted regular all-purpose
flour
2 teaspoons sugar
2 teaspoons salt
2 cups unsifted regular all-purpose
flour (more or less)
½ teaspoon soda (or more)

Combine water, starter, the 4 cups flour, salt, and sugar. Mix well, place in a crock, and leave at room temperature about 18 hours, or until sponge has doubled in size. (If you start at 3 p.m., you can begin next step about 9 a.m. the next day.) Stir in 1 cup of the remaining flour which has been mixed with the soda; the resulting dough will be very stiff. Turn dough out onto a floured board and knead, adding remaining 1 cup flour as needed. Knead until smooth—at least 8 minutes, until the dough cannot absorb any more flour.

Shape into two oblong loaves or one large round loaf. Place on a *lightly* greased cooky sheet, cover, and place in a warm place for 3 to 4 hours, or until nearly doubled in bulk. Just before baking, brush with water; make diagonal slashes in the top with a sharp knife or a single-edge razor. Place a shallow pan of hot water in the bottom of the oven. (For a more tender crust, do not place pan of water in oven, and brush unbaked loaf with salad oil or butter instead of water.) Bake in a hot oven (400°) until crust is a medium dark brown (about 45 minutes for the oblong loaves, 50 minutes for the large round loaf). For a heavier and tougher crust, remove loaf from oven 10 minutes before it is done; brush with salted water and return to a very hot oven (425°) for the remaining time.

WHOLE WHEAT SOURDOUGH FRENCH BREAD

The whole wheat flour gives Sourdough French Bread a light brown color and nut-like flavor.

Make Sourdough French Bread by either the long or the short method, replacing the 4 cups of unsifted regular all-purpose flour with 3 cups whole wheat flour and 1 cup regular all-purpose flour. Continue with remaining ingredients and technique as given, using regular all-purpose flour (about 2 cups, as indicated) when you add flour at kneading stage.

SOURDOUGH BANANA BREAD

This moist banana bread is ready to slice and serve as soon as it has cooled.

    ⅓ cup shortening
    1 cup sugar
    1 egg
    1 cup mashed banana
    1 cup starter
    2 cups regular all-purpose flour
        (sift before measuring)
    1 teaspoon salt
    1 teaspoon baking powder
    ½ teaspoon soda
    ¾ cup chopped walnuts

Cream together shortening and sugar; add egg, and mix until blended. Stir in banana and starter. Sift flour again with salt, baking powder, and soda.

Add flour mixture and walnuts to the first mixture, stirring just until blended. Pour into a greased 9 by 5-inch loaf pan.

Bake in a moderate oven (350°) for 1 hour 5 minutes, or until pick comes out clean. Cool thoroughly before slicing.

CORN FRENCH BREAD

Make the sponge exactly as stated in recipe for Sourdough French Bread (either method) using the 4 cups regular all-purpose flour. After sponge has risen, mix soda with 1 cup yellow corn meal (in place of 1 cup flour); stir into sponge. Continue as directed.

CINNAMON ROLLS

These light, tender pinwheel cinnamon rolls are best served hot from the oven. Or you can let them cool and glaze them with a powdered sugar icing.

    ½ cup starter
    1 cup undiluted evaporated milk
    2 cups unsifted regular all-purpose
        flour
    ¼ cup (⅛ lb.) soft butter
    3 tablespoons sugar
    1 egg
    1½ cups unsifted regular
        all-purpose flour (or more)
    ½ teaspoon soda
    1 teaspoon baking powder
    1 teaspoon salt
    2 tablespoons butter, melted
    ¼ cup brown sugar, firmly packed
    1½ teaspoons cinnamon
    ¼ cup raisins (optional)
        Melted butter

Combine starter, evaporated milk, and 2 cups flour in a large bowl; cover and leave at room temperature overnight. The next morning, beat together butter, sugar, and egg; blend into sourdough mixture. Combine the 1½ cups flour, soda, baking powder, and salt; mix with other mixture. Turn onto a floured board and knead until the surface is satiny and doesn't stick to board (add flour if necessary).

Place ball of dough in the center of board and roll out to a rectangle 8 inches by 16 inches. Brush surface with melted butter and sprinkle with a mixture of brown sugar and cinnamon (and raisins, if you wish). Roll up dough, starting on one of the long sides; cut roll at 1¾-inch intervals with a string or sharp knife. (You should have 9 rolls.) Dip top and bottom of each roll in melted butter, place in a square 9-inch pan, cover loosely, and let rise in a warm place for about 1 hour, or until nearly doubled. Bake in a moderately hot oven (375°) for 30 to 35 minutes or until crust is dark golden. Makes 9 large rolls.

This sourdough pan bread combines sourdough's tangy flavor with wheat germ in compact loaf.

SOURDOUGH PAN BREAD

By substituting flours, you can make wheat germ, corn meal, or oatmeal bread from this basic recipe.

1 cup starter
2½ cups water
5 cups unsifted regular all-purpose flour
3 tablespoons melted shortening
2 tablespoons sugar
1 tablespoon salt
1½ teaspoons soda
About 2½ cups unsifted regular all-purpose flour
Melted butter

In a large bowl, mix starter, water, and the 5 cups of flour; cover and leave 18 to 24 hours at room temperature. Then combine melted shortening, sugar, salt, and soda; add to first mixture, and stir vigorously until blended.

Turn out dough onto 2½ cups flour on a board; knead until satiny, adding more flour if needed. Divide dough in half; shape into loaves and place each in a buttered loaf pan (5 by 9 inches). Let rise in a warm place until nearly doubled (2 to 5 hours). Brush with melted butter. Bake in a hot oven (400°) for 45 minutes. Turn out of pan; cool. Makes 2 loaves.

VARIATIONS: Make substitutions for a portion of the first 5 cups flour. For wheat germ bread, use ⅔ cup wheat germ for ⅔ cup flour; for corn meal or oatmeal bread, use 1 cup corn meal or rolled oats for 1 cup flour.

SOURDOUGH BREAD STICKS

Make the dough as directed in Sourdough French Bread recipe (either method), but instead of shaping it into loaves, divide it in 2 balls. Roll each ball out on a floured board to a thickness of ½ inch. Slice dough in long strips, ½ inch wide, and roll each strip with your hands on a floured board to make them cylindrical. Brush with water and place about 1 inch apart on lightly greased baking sheet. Let rise in warm place for 30 minutes and bake in hot oven (400°) for 20 minutes or until browned.

HOLIDAY BREAD

Utilize your sourdough starter for holiday baking. This colorful braid is filled with almonds, candied cherries, and raisins. The flavor of sourdough is not distinguishable, but the total effect is a tasty bread with a tender crunchy crust.

    ¾ cup warm water
    ½ cup starter
    2 cups unsifted regular all-purpose
        flour
    ½ cup (¼ lb.) butter or margarine
    ½ cup sugar
    2 egg yolks
    1 cup unsifted regular all-purpose
        flour
    1 teaspoon salt
    ½ teaspoon soda
    ½ teaspoon cinnamon
    ½ teaspoon grated lemon peel
    ½ cup sliced almonds
    ½ cup raisins
    ½ cup coarsely chopped candied
        cherries
1 ¼ cups unsifted regular all-purpose
        flour (or more)
        Egg white

Mix water, starter, and 2 cups flour in a mixing bowl; cover and leave overnight at room tempera-

Use your sourdough starter for holiday baking. You can make this bread early and freeze it.

ture. The next morning, cream butter, sugar, and egg yolks together with electric mixer. Combine the 1 cup flour, salt, soda, cinnamon, and lemon peel; blend into creamed mixture. Blend in the almonds, raisins, and cherries. Mix this with sourdough mixture; turn out on a mound of the 1¼ cups flour; knead until surface is satiny and not sticky (add more flour if necessary).

Divide dough into thirds and roll each third on the board with your hands to form a strand about 18 inches long. Place strands on a greased cooky sheet and braid together to form a straight braid. Let rise in a warm place for about 2 hours. Paint with egg white. Bake in a moderate oven (350°) for 50 to 55 minutes or until a medium brown. Makes 1 loaf.

SOURDOUGH DATE LOAF

In this moist date loaf, the subtle tang of sourdough blends with the sweetness of sugar and dates.

    ½ cup starter
1 ½ cups unsifted regular all-purpose
        flour
    1 cup undiluted evaporated milk
    2 tablespoons sugar
    ¼ cup (⅛ lb.) butter or margarine
    ¾ cup brown sugar, firmly packed
    1 cup chopped dates
    ½ cup chopped walnuts
    2 eggs, beaten
    ½ cup quick-cooking rolled oats
    1 teaspoon baking powder
    ½ teaspoon soda
    ½ teaspoon salt

The night before, combine starter, flour, evaporated milk, and sugar; partially cover and leave at room temperature overnight. The next day, cream butter and brown sugar. Add dates and nuts; set aside. Combine eggs, rolled oats, baking powder, soda, and salt; stir into the sourdough mixture with date mixture. Turn into a greased loaf pan (5 by 9 inches) and let rise about 1 hour. Bake in a moderately hot oven (375°) for 1 hour. Cool for 10 minutes in pan, then remove from pan to cooling rack. Serve warm or cool. Makes 1 loaf.

Above (l. to r.) sourdough biscuits, French bread, starter, bread in final proofing, dough rising in bowl.

SOURDOUGH ENGLISH MUFFINS

You can bake your own sourdough English muffins while you prepare breakfast for your family or guests. Serve hot from the griddle, or split and toast them.

  ½ cup starter
  1 cup milk
2¾ cups unsifted regular all-purpose
     flour
  1 tablespoon sugar
  ¾ teaspoon salt
  ½ teaspoon soda
     About 3 tablespoons corn meal

In a large mixing bowl, combine starter, milk, and 2 cups of the flour; mix together with a large spoon, cover loosely, and set aside at room temperature for about 8 hours or overnight. Mix ½ cup of the flour, the sugar, salt, and soda; sprinkle over dough; thoroughly mix in. Turn this very stiff dough out onto a board floured with the remaining ¼ cup flour; knead for 2 to 3 minutes or until no longer sticky—add flour if necessary.

Roll dough out to a ¾-inch thickness. Use a 3-inch cutter (a 7-oz. tuna can with ends removed makes a good cutter) to cut out 12 muffins. Place muffins 1 inch apart on a cooky pan or waxed paper which has been sprinkled with corn meal. Sprinkle more corn meal over top. Cover with a cloth or waxed paper; set aside in a warm place to rise—about 45 minutes.

Bake on a lightly greased electric griddle set at 275°, or in a frying pan over medium heat, for 8 to 10 minutes per side, turn once. Serve warm from the griddle, or split and toast. Makes 12 muffins.

Sourdough Limpa Muffins are hearty, moist, and not too sweet—good with any meal.

SOURDOUGH LIMPA MUFFINS

This version of sourdough muffins is hearty and moist, and because the muffins are not too sweet, they are good with dinner as well as breakfast.

   1½ cups unsifted regular all-purpose
       flour
   ½ cup rye flour
   ½ cup brown sugar, firmly packed
    1 teaspoon salt
    1 teaspoon soda
    1 egg, slightly beaten
   ½ cup cultured buttermilk
   ½ cup salad oil
    2 teaspoons grated orange peel
   ¾ cup starter

In a bowl, mix together flours, brown sugar, salt, and soda. Make a well in the center. Blend egg, milk, and oil together; stir in orange peel and starter. Pour this mixture all at once into the flour

well. Stir just to moisten ingredients, with about 12 to 15 full circular strokes that scrape the bottom of the bowl; batter will still look lumpy.

Grease muffin cups or line with baking cup liners; fill about ⅔ full, and bake in a moderately hot oven (375°) for 30 to 35 minutes. Makes 12 to 15 muffins.

SOURDOUGH OATMEAL MUFFINS

Follow the recipe for Sourdough Limpa Muffins with the following changes: Substitute 1 cup regular rolled oats for the rye flour, and omit the orange peel.

SOURDOUGH BISCUITS

Serve these sourdough biscuits only hot with butter —they become very firm when cold.

   ½ cup starter
    1 cup milk
 2½ cups unsifted regular all-purpose
       flour
   ¾ teaspoon salt
    1 tablespoon sugar
    1 teaspoon baking powder (double
       acting)
     About ½ teaspoon soda
     Bacon grease or salad oil and
      butter

Mix the starter, milk, and 1 cup of the flour in a large bowl (the night before if you're serving the biscuits for breakfast; in the morning if you want them for dinner). Cover the bowl and keep at room temperature to let rise.

Turn this very soft dough out onto 1 cup flour on a bread board. Combine salt, sugar, baking powder, and soda with remaining ½ cup flour and sift over the top. With your hands, mix dry ingredients into the soft dough, kneading lightly to get correct consistency. Roll out to a ½-inch thickness. Cut out biscuits with a cutter, and dip each in either warm bacon grease or a mixture of half salad oil and half melted butter.

Place close together in a 9-inch square pan and set in a warm place to let rise for about ½ hour. Bake in a moderately hot oven (375°) for 30 to 35 minutes. Makes about 14 biscuits (2½-inch).

SOURDOUGH SCONES

For a breakfast treat, set the dough the night before, then shape and bake these scones in the morning. Or follow the refrigerator method outlined below, which leaves only the baking for morning.

> ½ cup starter
> ¾ cup milk
> 2¼ cups unsifted regular all-purpose
>   flour
> 3 tablespoons melted butter
> ¼ cup sugar
> ¾ teaspoon salt
> ½ teaspoon soda
> 3 tablespoons dried currants
>   Melted butter

In a large bowl mix the starter, milk, and 1½ cups of the flour. Cover with a cloth; leave at room temperature for about 8 hours or overnight. Pour the 3 tablespoons butter over top; mix in. In another bowl, mix together ½ cup of remaining flour, the sugar, salt, and soda; sprinkle over first mixture with the currants; blend thoroughly. Knead dough lightly on a board floured with the remaining ¼ cup flour until it loses stickiness. Roll into a 9-inch

square. Cut into nine 3-inch squares; dip each on both sides in melted butter and arrange in a 9-inch baking pan. Loosely cover pan; let rise in a warm place until nearly doubled, about 45 minutes. Bake in a moderately hot oven (375°) for about 35 minutes. Makes 9 scones.

REFRIGERATOR SCONES: Make as directed above, but start process early the day before. Shape scones that evening, let rise for 30 minutes; refrigerate up to 12 hours. Before baking, let scones rise again in a warm place for 30 minutes or until nearly doubled in size.

SOURDOUGH CORN BREAD

The sourdough flavor combines with the taste and texture of corn bread to give you new flavor in this old favorite. It is not started the night before, since here the purpose of the starter is only to give flavor and a reaction with the soda. Bake it in a frying pan and serve it in wedges.

> 1 cup starter
> 1½ cups yellow corn meal
> 1½ cups evaporated milk
> 2 eggs, beaten
> 2 tablespoons sugar
> ¼ cup (⅛ lb.) warm melted butter
> ½ teaspoon salt
>   About ¾ teaspoon soda

Thoroughly mix the starter, corn meal, evaporated milk, eggs, and sugar in a large bowl. Stir in melted butter, salt, and soda. Turn into a 10-inch greased frying pan and bake in a hot oven (450°) for 25 to 30 minutes. Serve hot.

CORN BREAD STICKS

Make Sourdough Corn Bread. Spoon batter into a buttered corn stick pan, filling each cup ⅔ full. Bake in a very hot oven (425°) for 20 minutes, or until it tests done.

QUICK BREADS

These are the breads you make without yeast, a group that includes a wide variety of loaves and little breads for all occasions. Almost all of them are particularly easy to make. Most of the loaves are heavily studded with fruits and nuts, making them moist and sweet. They keep well, and will usually improve in flavor and be easier to slice after they have been wrapped and stored for a day or more.

LEMON BREAD

Serve this bread for a special breakfast or with coffee or tea. It has a cake-like texture.

½ cup shortening
1 cup sugar
2 eggs, slightly beaten
1¼ cups regular all-purpose flour
    (sift before measuring)
1 teaspoon baking powder
½ teaspoon salt
½ cup milk
½ cup finely chopped nuts
    Grated peel of 1 lemon
¼ cup sugar
    Juice of 1 lemon

Cream shortening with sugar; mix in eggs. Sift flour again with baking powder and salt. Alternately add the flour mixture and the milk to shortening mixture, stirring constantly. Mix in the nuts and

Bake Applesauce Raisin Bread in a fluted mold, slice while hot; butter and serve.

lemon peel. Bake in a greased 5 by 9-inch loaf pan in a moderate oven (350°) for 1 hour. Combine the ¼ cup sugar with the lemon juice and pour over the top of the loaf when it comes from the oven. (You can poke a few holes in the top before pouring over the juice if you wish.) Makes 1 loaf.

CRUNCHY NUT BREAD

Finely ground almonds and pecans give this whole wheat bread its rough, crunchy texture.

½ cup blanched almonds
½ cup pecans
1 cup regular all-purpose flour
    (sift before measuring)
2 teaspoons baking powder
1 teaspoon salt
1 cup stone ground whole wheat
    flour
¾ cup sugar
1 teaspoon shortening
1 egg
1 cup milk

Grind almonds and pecans through the fine blade of the food chopper. Sift all-purpose flour again with baking powder and salt; stir in whole wheat flour. Cream together sugar and shortening until crumbly; beat in egg. Gradually add dry ingredients to egg mixture alternately with milk, beating until smooth. Stir in nuts. Pour into a greased 9 by 5-inch loaf pan and let stand 20 minutes. Bake in a moderately slow oven (325°) for 1 hour and 15 minutes. Cool slightly and turn out of pan. Makes 1 loaf.

HONEY PINEAPPLE BREAD

This crunchy, coarse-textured bread has lots of pineapple and whole bran flavor.

    2 tablespoons salad oil
    1 cup honey
    1 egg, slightly beaten
    2 cups unsifted regular all-purpose
        flour
    2 teaspoons baking powder
    ¾ teaspoon salt
    1 cup whole bran
    1 cup pineapple juice
    ¾ cup chopped walnuts

In a bowl blend together well the salad oil, honey, and egg. Stir in the flour, baking powder, salt, whole bran, and pineapple juice, mixing just until dry ingredients are moistened. Fold in the nuts. Pour batter into a greased 5 by 9-inch bread loaf pan and bake in a moderate oven (350°) for 1 hour or until cake tester comes out clean. Makes 1 loaf.

APPLESAUCE RAISIN BREAD

If the whole loaf of this spicy bread doesn't disappear the first time you serve it, butter and toast slices when you serve it a second time.

    1 egg, slightly beaten
    1 cup applesauce
    ¼ cup (⅛ lb.) melted butter or
        margarine
    ½ cup granulated sugar
    ¼ cup brown sugar, firmly packed
    2 cups unsifted regular all-purpose
        flour
    2 teaspoons baking powder
    ¾ teaspoon salt
    ½ teaspoon soda
    ½ teaspoon cinnamon
    1 teaspoon nutmeg
    ½ cup seedless raisins
    1 cup coarsely chopped pecans
        or walnuts

In a bowl, combine the egg, applesauce, melted butter, granulated sugar, and brown sugar, blending well. Stir in the flour, baking powder, salt, soda, cinnamon, and nutmeg. Stir until smooth. Stir in the raisins and chopped nuts. Turn batter into a well-greased 5 by 9-inch loaf pan, or fluted mold with tube that holds about 1 quart. Bake in a moderate oven (350°) for 1 hour. Cool, and frost with light powdered sugar frosting, if you wish. This quick bread slices best the second day. Makes 1 large loaf.

OATMEAL APPLESAUCE LOAF

In this bread, applesauce supplies both liquid and flavor.

    4 tart apples, peeled, cored,
        and sliced
    ⅓ cup water
    ⅓ cup granulated sugar
    ⅔ cup brown sugar, firmly packed
    2 eggs
    1½ cups regular all-purpose flour
        (sift before measuring)
    1 teaspoon baking powder
    1 teaspoon soda
    1½ teaspoons salt
    1 teaspoon cinnamon
    ½ teaspoon nutmeg
    ⅓ cup melted shortening
    1½ cups rolled oats
    1 cup seedless raisins
    ½ cup coarsely chopped walnuts

In a covered saucepan, simmer apples in water for 15 minutes, or until apples are tender; then add granulated sugar and continue cooking until sugar dissolves. Mash apples with potato masher until smooth; cool.

Beat together the brown sugar and eggs until smooth; add 1 cup of the applesauce. Sift flour again with baking powder, soda, salt, cinnamon, and nutmeg into egg mixture; blend thoroughly. Stir in melted shortening, rolled oats, raisins, and nuts. Spoon batter into a well-greased 5 by 9-inch loaf pan. Bake in a moderate oven (350°) for 1 hour. Makes 1 loaf.

RAISIN OATMEAL BREAD

This unusual bread requires neither eggs nor fat. Let the dough stand in the loaf pan about 20 minutes before baking; it will develop a better texture.

1 cup regular all-purpose flour
(sift before measuring)
1 cup rye flour
(sift before measuring)
1 teaspoon baking powder
1 teaspoon salt
1 teaspoon soda
1 cup rolled oats
¼ cup sugar
½ cup molasses
1¼ cups buttermilk
1 cup raisins
½ cup chopped walnuts

Combine all-purpose and rye flours, and sift them again together with baking powder, salt, and soda. Stir in the oats and sugar. Gradually add molasses and buttermilk, and beat until mixture is smooth. Stir in raisins and walnuts. Pour into a greased 9 by 5-inch loaf pan. Let stand at room temperature 20 minutes. Bake in a moderate oven (350°) for 1 hour. Cool and turn out of pan. Makes 1 loaf.

CHERRY FIG BREAD

You start with prepared pancake mix to make this unusual fruit bread. It's baked in juice cans. Serve the bread rounds with luncheon salad.

1½ cups prepared pancake mix
½ cup brown sugar, well packed
1 egg, well beaten
1⅓ cups milk
Grated peel of 1 lemon
1 cup rolled oats
⅔ cup chopped dried figs
½ cup chopped candied cherries
3 tablespoons salad oil
Thin powdered sugar icing
(optional)

You'll need 7 frozen juice cans (6 oz. size); grease them well. Blend together the pancake mix and sugar. Lightly stir in egg, milk, lemon peel, rolled oats, figs, cherries, and salad oil. Spoon into the 7 greased cans. Bake in a moderate oven (350°) about 30 minutes. (Or bake in a greased waxed-paper-lined 5 by 9-inch loaf pan about 1 hour.) Remove from pans immediately, running a knife along side of each to loosen. While bread is still warm, drizzle with thin powdered sugar icing, if you wish.

DATE-NUT LOAF

You won't taste a distinct cheese flavor, but Cheddar lends interesting character to this bread and seems to enhance the nut and fruit flavors.

¾ cup boiling water
½ pound pitted dates, finely cut
2 tablespoons butter or margarine
1¾ cups regular all-purpose flour
(sift before measuring)
¼ teaspoon salt
1 teaspoon soda
½ cup sugar
1 egg, well beaten
1 cup shredded Cheddar cheese
¾ to 1 cup walnuts

Pour boiling water over the dates and butter; let stand about 5 minutes, until all the butter is melted and the mixture has cooled. Sift flour again with the salt, soda, and sugar into a bowl. Stir in the date mixture, beaten egg, cheese, and walnuts. Stir only until well blended. Pour into a well-buttered loaf pan (9 by 5 inches). Bake in a moderately slow oven (325°) for 50 to 60 minutes. Turn out on a rack to cool. Wrap well in foil or clear plastic wrap to store. Makes 1 loaf.

PORTUGUESE HONEY BREAD

While still warm from the oven, loaves of Portuguese honey bread can be sliced and served. Once cool, however, the loaves become very hard, and must mellow for several days before they soften again. The bread has a fine, dense texture and, like fruit cake, it keeps very well; but it contains only a small quantity of fruits and nuts. It is very liberally spiced, and has a rich aroma.

You might like to keep this bread on hand ready to serve during the holidays. It is excellent served in the traditional Portuguese fashion, thinly sliced, with cups of hot tea. But it is also a good choice to offer with eggnog and other holiday punches. This recipe makes three loaves, some to keep and some to give, as you wish.

2⅓ cups (1 lb. and ⅓ cup) soft butter
1½ cups light molasses
2¾ cups sugar
⅔ cup honey
⅓ cup cold mashed potatoes
⅓ cup sweet sherry
¾ cup chopped candied fruit
¼ cup chopped candied citron
1 cup broken walnuts
1½ teaspoons ground cloves
4 teaspoons anise seed
3⅔ tablespoons cinnamon
½ teaspoon black pepper
1 teaspoon soda
13 cups regular all-purpose flour
    (sift before measuring)

Cream butter, molasses, sugar, and honey until fluffy. Blend in potatoes, sherry, candied fruit, citron, walnuts, cloves, anise, cinnamon, pepper, and soda. Mix flour well with the batter. Butter and line the bottoms of 3 loaf pans (each 5 by 9 inches) with waxed paper and butter again. Divide the batter equally among the pans; smooth tops with a spoon or spatula. Bake in a very slow oven (250°) for 3 hours. Cool in pans on wire racks for 10 minutes. Turn loaves from pans and remove and discard the paper. Cool completely on racks (or slice and serve while still warm) then wrap airtight in foil.

Age the bread (both cut sections and whole loaves) at room temperature for at least 5 days; it will keep several months if sealed (or resealed). If you wish to freeze the loaves for longer storage, let them mature 5 days before freezing. Makes 3 loaves.

SWEET CORN BREAD

Delightful when hot, this sweet corn bread is also tasty and tender after cooling.

¾ cup sugar
½ cup salad oil
2 eggs, beaten
1½ cups regular all-purpose flour
    (sift before measuring)
3 teaspoons baking powder
⅛ teaspoon salt
1½ cups yellow corn meal
1 cup milk

Blend sugar and salad oil. Mix in eggs. Sift flour again with baking powder, and salt; add corn meal. Blend dry ingredients with the creamed mixture alternately with milk. Pour into a greased, floured 9-inch square pan. Bake in a hot oven (400°) for 30 minutes. Makes 6 servings.

HERB CORN STICKS

These light textured corn sticks have a subtle herb flavor.

1⅔ cups regular all-purpose flour
    (sift before measuring)
3 teaspoons baking powder
½ teaspoon salt
2 tablespoons sugar
¾ cup corn meal
½ teaspoon crumbled dried marjoram
½ teaspoon thyme
1 egg
1½ cups milk
¼ cup (⅛ lb.) butter or margarine

Sift flour again with baking powder, salt, and sugar. Stir in corn meal, marjoram, and thyme. In another bowl, beat egg; stir in milk and melted butter, then add all at once to the dry ingredients and stir just until mixture is moistened.

Spoon into well-greased corn stick pans, filling about three-fourths full. Bake in a hot oven (425°) for 20 minutes, or until golden brown. Makes about 21 medium-sized corn sticks.

IRISH SODA BREAD

This recipe, with its variations, comes from Dublin. Gill and pound measurements have been changed to cups, heaping spoons to standard measurements, and the recipes generally adapted to our ingredients; but the result tastes and looks like the original. The basic recipe makes two loaves about 8 inches in diameter; the breads are delicious either warm from the oven or cold.

As you can see by its variations, this is a versatile bread; you can sweeten it with sugar and fruit, or vary its flavor with different grains.

        4 cups unsifted regular all-purpose
            flour
        1 teaspoon salt
        3 teaspoons baking powder
        1 teaspoon soda
        ¼ cup sugar (optional)
        ⅛ teaspoon cardamom or coriander
            (optional)
        ¼ cup (⅛ lb.) butter or margarine
        1 egg
        1¾ cups buttermilk

Combine in a large bowl the flour, salt, baking powder, soda, sugar and spice, if used. Add butter or margarine, and cut in with a pastry blender or two knives until crumbly. Beat egg slightly and mix with buttermilk; add to dry ingredients and stir until blended. Turn out on a floured board and knead until smooth, 2 to 3 minutes.

Divide dough in half, and shape each into a round loaf; place each loaf in an 8-inch cake or pie pan. Press down until dough fills pans. With a sharp knife, cut crosses on tops of loaves, about

Currant soda bread is cut in wedges to serve; whole wheat soda bread is shown at left.

½ inch deep in the middle. Bake in a moderately hot oven (375°) for 35 to 40 minutes. Makes 1 loaf.

CURRANT OR RAISIN SODA BREAD

Follow basic recipe for Irish Soda Bread, including the sugar; omit the cardamom or coriander. Add 2 cups currants or raisins to the flour mixture with 1¼ teaspoons caraway seed (optional). Blend with egg and buttermilk and proceed as directed in basic recipe.

WHOLE WHEAT SODA BREAD

Substitute 2 cups whole wheat flour for 2 cups of the all-purpose flour in the basic recipe for Irish Soda Bread. You might add 1 to 2 cups raisins or chopped dates, if you wish; mix in with the dry ingredients before adding the liquid.

FRESH APPLE FRUIT LOAF

The fragrances of fresh apples and blended spices dominate in this quick loaf bread. It is packed full of fruits and nuts to give a crunchy texture.

  1 cup brown sugar, firmly packed
 ½ cup salad oil
  2 tablespoons sherry
  1 teaspoon vanilla
  1 cup raisins
  1 cup coarsely cut mixed
      candied fruit
  1 cup chopped nuts
  1 cup pitted fresh dates cut in
      small pieces
1½ cups coarsely shredded peeled
      raw apples
  2 teaspoons soda
  2 cups regular all-purpose flour
      (sift before measuring)
 ½ teaspoon salt
 ¼ teaspoon ground cinnamon
 ¼ teaspoon nutmeg

In a large mixing bowl, mix together brown sugar, salad oil, sherry, and vanilla. Stir in raisins, candied fruit, nuts, and dates. Stir in apples mixed with the soda. Sift flour again into mixture with salt, cinnamon, and nutmeg. Stir to blend thoroughly. Turn into a greased and floured loaf pan (5 by 9 inches). Bake in a moderate oven (350°) for 1 hour, 25 minutes, or until toothpick inserted in center comes out clean. Allow loaf to cool in pan for about 3 minutes; turn onto wire rack to continue cooling. Makes 1 loaf.

RIESKA

The wheatless bread called *rieska* is a traditional favorite in northern Finland and Lapland. You can make it quickly, and it's best served freshly made, still hot, spread with butter. Serve it as you would any quick hot bread like biscuits or muffins. You can buy barley flour in health food stores; rye flour is available in most supermarkets. You may want to vary the recipe below by using half of each.

  2 cups barley flour or rye flour
 ¾ teaspoon salt
  2 teaspoons sugar
  2 teaspoons baking powder
  1 cup undiluted evaporated milk
      or light cream
  2 tablespoons butter, melted

In a bowl combine the flour with the salt, sugar, and baking powder. Stir in the milk or cream and the melted butter until a smooth dough forms. Turn the dough out onto a well-buttered cooky sheet, dust your hands lightly with flour and pat the dough out to make a circle about 14 inches in diameter and ½ inch thick.

Prick all over with a fork, and bake in a very hot oven (450°) for 10 minutes or until lightly browned. Serve immediately cut in pie-shaped wedges and spread with plenty of butter. Makes 8 to 10 pieces.

ALMOND TEA BREAD

This quick almond loaf bread is really sweet enough to be classified as a cake. It is like a pound-cake filled with toasted, slivered almonds; yet you can slice it, spread it with butter, and serve it with coffee or tea. To make almond toast, slice, butter, and place bread under the broiler just until the butter melts and top crisps.

If you don't mind a few crumbs, you can slice

a warm loaf of it a little thicker than usual. To get clean-cut slices, cool thoroughly before cutting.

> ½ cup (¼ lb.) butter
> 1 cup sugar
> 1 egg
> 2 cups regular all-purpose flour
>   (sift before measuring)
> ¼ teaspoon baking powder
> ¼ teaspoon soda
> ¼ teaspoon salt
> ½ cup light cream
> ¼ teaspoon almond extract
> ½ cup slivered almonds, toasted

In a bowl cream the butter until light; blend in the sugar. Mix in the egg until well blended. Sift flour again with the baking powder, soda, and salt. Add the flour mixture alternately with the cream to the creamed mixture, mixing until well blended. Stir in the almond extract and the toasted slivered almonds. Pour into a greased loaf pan (about 9 by 5 inches). Bake in a moderately slow oven (325°) for 60 to 70 minutes, or until cake tester comes out clean. Cool in pan for a few minutes, then turn out on a wire rack to continue cooling. Makes 1 loaf.

BUTTERSCOTCH NUT BREAD

Sesame seed with sugar and spices forms the topping on this rich, delicious bread.

> 2 tablespoons sesame seed
> 2 tablespoons sugar
> ¼ teaspoon cinnamon
> ¼ teaspoon nutmeg
> 2 cups regular all-purpose flour
>   (sift before measuring)
> 1 teaspoon baking powder
> ½ teaspoon soda
> 1 teaspoon salt
> 2 eggs
> 1 cup brown sugar, firmly packed
> 3 tablespoons melted butter or
>   margarine
> 1 cup buttermilk
> ⅔ cup chopped filberts or walnuts

Combine the sesame seed with the sugar, cinnamon, and nutmeg; set aside. Sift flour again with the baking powder, soda, and salt. In a large bowl, beat the eggs slightly; add the brown sugar and melted butter and mix well. Add the flour mixture alternately with the buttermilk, stirring just until well blended. Stir in the nuts. Pour into a well-greased loaf pan (5 by 9 inches). Sprinkle the top with the sesame seed and sugar mixture. Bake in a moderate oven (350°) for about 1 hour, or until bread starts to come away from sides of pan. Cool slightly, then remove bread from pan. Serve warm or cooled. Makes 1 loaf.

APRICOT NUT BREAD

For this bread you sift non-fat dry milk with the dry ingredients so you can use fruit juices for the liquid.

> 1 cup dried apricots
> 2 cups water
> 1 cup sugar
> 2 tablespoons butter or margarine
> 1 egg
>   Grated peel of 1 orange
> 3½ cups regular all-purpose flour
>   (sift before measuring)
> 2 teaspoons baking powder
> 1 teaspoon soda
> 1 teaspoon salt
> ½ cup non-fat dry milk
> ¾ cup apricot liquid
> ½ cup orange juice
> ¼ cup chopped walnuts

Cover the apricots with the water and cook until apricots are tender but not mushy; drain off liquid and save. Cream together sugar and butter; beat in egg and grated orange peel. Sift flour again with baking powder, soda, salt, and non-fat dry milk. Add to creamed mixture alternately with apricot and orange juices.

Chop apricots and stir into batter with the walnut meats. Spoon into two greased 3½ by 7½-inch loaf pans. Bake in a moderate oven (350°) for 40 to 45 minutes, or until bread springs back when touched in the center. Makes 2 small loaves.

Carrot bread, baked in a long, rounded cake mold and (background) in two 1-pound cans.

CARROT-COCONUT BREAD

The moist, fruity quality of this bread is due largely to the carrots. You won't taste them as a vegetable.

    3 eggs
    ½ cup salad oil
    1 teaspoon vanilla
    2 cups finely shredded carrots
    2 cups packaged grated coconut
    1 cup raisins
    1 cup chopped walnuts
    2 cups unsifted regular all-purpose
        flour
    ½ teaspoon salt
    1 teaspoon soda
    1 teaspoon baking powder
    1 teaspoon cinnamon
    1 cup sugar

In a large bowl, beat the eggs until light. Stir in salad oil and vanilla; add carrots, coconut, raisins, and nuts, and mix until well blended. Combine the flour, salt, soda, baking powder, cinnamon, and sugar; sift into the first mixture. Stir just until well blended. Spoon into a 9 by 5-inch loaf pan that has been well buttered and dusted with flour. Bake in a moderate oven (350°) for about 1 hour, or until it tests done. Remove from pan and cool thoroughly. Its flavor and texture improve if wrapped and refrigerated for several days. Makes 1 loaf.

CARROT BREAD

Carrot bread has a spicy flavor, fine texture, and crisp outer crusts.

    4 eggs
    2 cups sugar
    1¼ cups salad oil
    3 cups unsifted regular all-purpose
        flour
    2 teaspoons baking powder
    1½ teaspoons soda
    ¼ teaspoon salt
    2 teaspoons cinnamon
    2 cups finely shredded raw carrots

Beat the eggs, and add the sugar gradually, beating until thick. Add the oil gradually and continue beating until thoroughly combined. Stir in the flour, baking powder, soda, salt, and cinnamon until mixture is smooth. Stir in the carrots until blended well. Turn into two well-greased 5 by 9-inch loaf pans or four well-greased 1-pound cans, filling them no more than ⅔ full. Bake the bread in a moderate oven (350°) for 1 hour for large loaf or 45 minutes for small loaves or until a cake tester comes out clean. Makes 2 loaves.

ORANGE NUT BREAD

When tangerines are in season, you may want to substitute tangerine peel for the orange peel in this chewy bread.

    ¾ cup orange peel, pared from 3
        large oranges with potato peeler
    1 cup water
    1 cup granulated sugar
    1 cup brown sugar, firmly packed
    1 tablespoon butter or margarine
    1 egg
    1 cup finely chopped walnuts
    3½ cups unsifted regular all-purpose
        flour
    3 teaspoons baking powder
    ½ teaspoon salt
    1 cup milk

Put orange peel and water into electric blender, and whirl at high speed until peel is cut into fine pieces (or put just the peel through food chopper with finest blade three times or until peel is fine, then combine with water). Put the orange-water mixture and the 1 cup granulated sugar into a pan and bring to a boil. Boil, stirring, until reduced to 1 cup, about 15 minutes. Set aside.

In a bowl, combine the brown sugar and butter with a fork until butter is like coarse crumbs. Stir in the egg, walnuts, and orange peel mixture, mixing until well blended. Sift the flour, baking powder, and salt together, and add alternately to the mixture with the milk, mixing just until combined. Turn into a well-buttered 5 by 9-inch loaf pan or into three buttered cans (1 lb. size), and bake in a moderate oven (350°) for 45 minutes for small loaves or 1 hour for large loaf, or until cake tester comes out clean. Cool and slice. Makes 1 large loaf or 3 small ones.

CRANBERRY-ORANGE BREAD

This moist, compact bread is delicately sweet and orange flavored. And you'll find a plump cranberry here and there.

    1 cup sugar
    3 tablespoons butter or margarine
    1 egg
      Grated peel of 1 large orange
    3 cups whole wheat flour
    2 teaspoons baking powder
    1 teaspoon soda
    1 teaspoon salt
    1 can (1 lb.) whole cranberry sauce
      Juice of 1 large orange
    1 cup broken walnuts
    ½ cup wheat germ

Cream together thoroughly the sugar and butter, and beat in the egg; blend in orange peel. Blend flour with baking powder, soda, and salt; set aside. Drain cranberries. Reserving cranberries, add orange juice to the cranberry syrup. Add this juice combination alternately with the dry ingredients to the creamed mixture, blending after each addition. Stir in cranberries, walnuts, and wheat germ. Turn into a large (5 by 9 inches), greased loaf pan; bake in a moderate oven (350°) for 60 minutes, or until it tests done. Cool before slicing. Makes 1 loaf.

ORANGE GUMDROP DATE BREAD

Jewel-like bits of orange gumdrops stud this moist, fine-textured loaf. If you use concentrated frozen orange juice, dilute it with only two cans of water instead of the usual three.

    1 cup hot water
    1½ cups pitted fresh dates,
      cut into small pieces
    ¾ cup granulated sugar
    ¾ cup brown sugar, firmly packed
    ½ cup (¼ lb.) soft butter or
      margarine
    2 eggs
    1 cup orange juice
    2 cups cut-up orange gumdrops
    1 teaspoon grated orange peel
    4 cups regular all-purpose flour
      (sift before measuring)
    2 teaspoons baking powder
    2 teaspoons soda
    1 teaspoon salt

Pour hot water over dates; allow to stand 15 minutes. In a large mixing bowl, cream together thoroughly granulated sugar, brown sugar, and butter or margarine. Beat in eggs, one at a time. Add orange juice. Stir in dates (including water), gumdrops, and grated orange peel. Sift flour again into mixing bowl along with baking powder, soda, and salt. Stir to combine thoroughly.

Divide mixture evenly into 2 well-greased 9 by 5-inch loaf pans. Bake in a moderate oven (350°) for 1 hour or until a toothpick inserted in center comes out clean. Cool loaves in pans for about 3 minutes, then turn out on a wire rack to continue cooling. Makes 2 loaves.

WHOLE WHEAT BANANA BREAD

Whole wheat flour enriches the flavor of this moist banana bread, which has a light, cake-like texture.

½ cup (¼ lb.) butter or margarine
1 cup sugar
2 eggs, slightly beaten
3 medium-sized bananas
    (1 cup mashed)
1 cup regular all-purpose flour
    (sift before measuring)
½ teaspoon salt
1 teaspoon soda
1 cup whole wheat flour
⅓ cup hot water
½ cup chopped walnuts

Melt butter and blend in sugar. Mix in beaten eggs and mashed bananas, blending until smooth. Sift all-purpose flour again with salt and soda. Stir in whole wheat flour. Add dry ingredients alternately with hot water. Stir in chopped nut meats. Turn into a greased, 9 by 5-inch loaf pan. Bake in a moderately slow oven (325°) for 1 hour and 10 minutes. Makes 1 loaf.

BANANA COCONUT TEA BREAD

You accent the coconut flavor when you toast flaked coconut before you fold it into the banana-moist batter for this bread.

⅓ cup soft butter or margarine
⅔ cup sugar
2 eggs
3 tablespoons milk
1 teaspoon lemon juice
½ teaspoon almond extract
2 cups regular all-purpose flour
    (sift before measuring)
1 teaspoon baking powder
½ teaspoon soda
½ teaspoon salt
1 cup mashed ripe bananas
1 cup toasted flaked coconut

In a large mixing bowl, cream together butter and sugar. Beat in eggs, one at a time. Stir in milk, lemon juice, and almond extract. Sift flour again into mixing bowl along with baking powder, soda, and salt; mix thoroughly. Stir in bananas; fold in toasted coconut. Pour into a well-greased loaf pan (5 by 9 inches). Bake in a moderate oven (350°) for 55 minutes, or until a toothpick inserted in center comes out clean. Cool in pan a few minutes; turn out on wire rack to continue cooling. Makes 1 loaf.

NOTE: To toast coconut, sprinkle on a baking sheet and place in a moderate oven (350°) or under broiler until lightly browned, stirring occasionally.

STOLLEN

German stollen is familiar to most as a yeast bread. But this quick version, too, is a traditional recipe from Germany.

Vanilla sugar, the perfumed, sparkling topping for stollen, must be made ahead: Bury a split vanilla bean in 1 cup sugar and cover container tightly. Let stand for 2 or 3 days at room temperature.

2½ cups unsifted regular all-purpose flour
2 teaspoons baking powder
¾ cup sugar
½ teaspoon salt
¼ teaspoon mace
⅛ teaspoon cardamom
¾ cup ground blanched almonds
½ cup (¼ lb.) cold butter
1 cup cottage cheese, whirled
    smooth in a blender or forced
    through a wire strainer
1 egg
½ teaspoon vanilla
¼ teaspoon almond extract
2 tablespoons rum
    (or 1½ tablespoons water and
    ½ teaspoon rum flavoring)
½ cup currants
½ cup golden raisins
¼ cup chopped candied lemon peel
3 tablespoons melted butter
2 tablespoons vanilla sugar
    (see directions above)

This quick-bread version of stollen is more moist than yeast kind and easier to make. It freezes well.

Combine flour, baking powder, sugar, salt, mace, cardamom, and almonds. Cut in butter with a pastry blender until mixture resembles coarse crumbs.

Blend cottage cheese, egg, vanilla, almond extract, rum, currants, raisins, and lemon peel; stir into flour mixture until all ingredients are moistened. Mold dough into a ball, place on a floured board, and knead 6 to 10 turns or until dough is smooth.

Roll dough out on a floured board to form an oval about 8½ by 10 inches. With rolling pin lightly crease dough just off center, parallel to the 10-inch side. Brush dough with 1 tablespoon of the melted butter. Fold smaller section over the larger. Place on an ungreased baking sheet which is covered with brown paper. Bake in a moderate oven (350°) for about 45 minutes or until crust is well browned and bread tests done in center. Brush with remaining butter; sprinkle with vanilla sugar.

Serve warm, or cool on a wire rack. Wrap airtight to mellow for 2 to 3 days, or freeze. To reheat, wrap loaf in foil and place in a moderate oven (350°) for 30 minutes. Slice to serve. Makes 1 loaf.

Pecan Sour Cream Coffee Cake, served warm or cold, is delicious accompaniment to coffee.

PECAN SOUR CREAM COFFEE CAKE

This moist cake with a baked-on topping can be served as a bread for breakfast or as a dessert. It keeps well when tightly covered.

   ½ cup (¼ lb.) butter or margarine
   1 cup granulated sugar
   3 eggs
   2 cups regular all-purpose flour
      (sift before measuring)
   1 teaspoon baking powder
   1 teaspoon soda
   ¼ teaspoon salt
   1 cup sour cream
   ½ cup golden raisins

PECAN TOPPING:
   ¾ cup brown sugar, firmly packed
   1 tablespoon flour
   1 teaspoon cinnamon
   2 tablespoons butter or margarine
   1 cup chopped pecans

In the large bowl of your electric mixer, cream together butter and sugar. Add eggs, one at a time, beating well after each addition. Sift flour again with baking powder, soda, and salt; add to creamed mixture alternately with sour cream, making about 3 equal additions of each and blending after each addition. Sprinkle raisins over the top and stir in.

Spread mixture in a greased baking pan (13 by 9 by 2 inches). Sprinkle with pecan topping, made as follows: Combine the brown sugar, flour, and cinnamon; mix together; cut in butter until the consistency of corn meal; mix in the chopped pecans.

Bake in a moderate oven (350°, or 325° for a glass pan) about 30 minutes or until it tests done. Cut in squares and serve either warm or cold. Makes 12 servings.

RAISIN-FILLED COFFEE CAKE

In this coffee cake, a pale gold, sugary crust hides a rich raisin-nut filling.

FILLING:
   1 tablespoon cornstarch
   ½ cup water
   ½ cup chopped walnuts
   ½ cup sugar
   1 cup raisins
     Grated peel and juice of 1 small
      lemon

BATTER:
   2 cups regular all-purpose flour
      (sift before measuring)
   2 teaspoons baking powder
   ½ teaspoon salt
   ¼ cup granulated sugar
   ½ cup brown sugar, firmly packed
   ½ cup (¼ lb.) butter or margarine
   ½ teaspoon vanilla
   2 eggs
   ½ cup milk
   2 tablespoons melted butter
   ¼ teaspoon cinnamon
   2 tablespoons sugar

In a saucepan, dissolve cornstarch in water. Add walnuts, sugar, raisins, lemon peel, and lemon juice. Bring to a boil over medium heat, stirring constantly. Cool while you prepare the cake batter.

Sift flour again with baking powder and salt. Cream together granulated sugar, brown sugar, and butter. Add vanilla. Add eggs and beat mixture until light and fluffy. Add flour and milk alternately, stirring after each addition. Spread half the batter in the bottom of a greased 8-inch square baking pan. Cover with raisin filling, and spread remaining batter carefully over filling. Brush with melted butter. Combine cinnamon with the 2 tablespoons sugar and sprinkle over batter. Bake in a moderate oven (350°) for about 30 minutes. Cool and cut in slices or squares. Makes 8 to 10 servings.

ORANGE COFFEE CAKE

The crisp, baked-on sugar topping adds additional orange flavor to this moist coffee cake, good warm or cold. The cake is sweetened with syrup instead of sugar.

> 2 cups regular all-purpose flour
>   (sift before measuring)
> ½ teaspoon salt
> 1 tablespoon baking powder
> ½ cup light corn syrup
> 1 teaspoon grated orange peel
> ½ cup orange juice
> ¼ cup melted butter, margarine,
>   or shortening
> 2 eggs, well beaten
> 1 teaspoon vanilla
>   Topping (recipe follows)

Sift flour again with salt and baking powder into a mixing bowl. Combine corn syrup, orange peel, orange juice, and melted butter; mix thoroughly with dry ingredients. Stir in eggs and vanilla. Pour into a greased and floured 8-inch square baking pan. Sprinkle topping over batter.

Bake in a hot oven (400°) for 30 minutes or until cake begins to pull away from edge of pan. Serve warm or cold. Makes 6 to 8 servings.

TOPPING: Combine 2 tablespoons grated orange peel, ½ cup sugar, 1 teaspoon cinnamon, and 1 tablespoon melted butter.

BUTTERMILK COFFEE CAKE

The topping for this cake requires a minimum of effort—it is simply a portion of the mixture of the first six ingredients of the cake combined with walnuts.

> 2¼ cups regular all-purpose flour
>   (sift before measuring)
> ½ teaspoon salt
> ½ teaspoon cinnamon
> 1 cup brown sugar, firmly packed
> ¾ cup granulated sugar
> ¾ cup salad oil
> ½ cup walnuts, coarsely chopped
> 1 teaspoon cinnamon
> 1 teaspoon soda
> 1 teaspoon baking powder
> 1 egg, slightly beaten
> 1 cup buttermilk

Sift flour again with salt and the ½ teaspoon cinnamon into large bowl of electric mixer. Add brown sugar, granulated sugar, and salad oil. Mix on medium speed until well-blended and feathery. Take out ¾ cup of this mixture for the topping; add nuts and the 1 teaspoon cinnamon and mix; set aside.

To the remaining mixture, add soda, baking powder, egg, and buttermilk; mix until smooth. Spoon mixture into a buttered pan (9 by 13 by 2 inches) and level off the top. Sprinkle the reserved topping evenly over the top and lightly press in with the back of a spoon. Bake in a moderate oven (350°, or 325° for glass pan) for 25 to 30 minutes or until it tests done. Cut in squares; serve warm. Makes 12 servings.

DANISH APPLE COCONUT COFFEE CAKE

This tender cake, studded with apples and topped with sliced almonds and sugar, is delightful served still warm from the oven for breakfast or brunch.

    ¾ cup butter or margarine
    1 cup sugar
    3 eggs
    1½ cups regular all-purpose flour
        (sift before measuring)
    2 teaspoons baking powder
    ¼ teaspoon salt
    ½ cup cold milk
    1¼ cups shredded coconut
    2 large tart apples, peeled and diced
    ¼ cup sliced almonds
    2 tablespoons sugar

Cream the butter and the 1 cup sugar until smooth. Stir in the eggs, blending very well. Sift flour again with the baking powder and salt, adding it to the creamed mixture alternately with the milk. Blend until smooth. Stir in the coconut, then fold in the apples. Pour into a well-greased 9 by 12-inch baking dish; sprinkle with the almonds, then with the 2 tablespoons sugar. Bake in a moderate oven (350°) for 30 to 35 minutes, or until cake springs back when lightly touched. Makes 12 squares.

LEMON-WALNUT COFFEE CAKE

Lemon provides an unusual flavoring in a coffee cake that calls for walnuts in the cake and in the topping.

    2 cups biscuit mix
    ½ cup chopped walnuts
    1 egg, slightly beaten
    ½ cup milk
    ½ cup brown sugar, firmly packed
    3 tablespoons melted butter or
        margarine
    1 tablespoon lemon juice
    2 teaspoons grated lemon peel
    Walnut Topping (recipe follows)

In a medium-sized bowl, combine biscuit mix and walnuts. Combine egg, milk, brown sugar, and melted butter. Add to mix, and stir just until moistened; blend in lemon juice and peel. Turn into a greased 8-inch square pan.

Sprinkle topping over batter. Bake in a hot oven (400°) for 30 minutes, or until golden brown. Makes 9 servings.

WALNUT TOPPING: Blend together until crumbly ½ cup chopped walnuts, 1 cup crushed cornflakes, ¼ cup sugar, ½ teaspoon cinnamon, and 2 tablespoons melted butter or margarine.

BLUEBERRY COFFEE CAKE

This blueberry-studded cake is best served warm, just out of the oven. But you can reheat it by spreading cooled pieces with butter and placing them in a moderate oven for about 8 minutes. You can also place buttered pieces under the broiler and lightly toast them.

    ⅔ cup butter or margarine
    1 cup sugar
    3 eggs, separated
    3 cups regular all-purpose flour
        (sift before measuring)
    2 teaspoons baking powder
    ¼ teaspoon salt
    1 cup milk
    1 package (10 oz.) sweetened, frozen
        blueberries, thawed and drained
    4 tablespoons brown sugar

Cream together butter and sugar, blend in egg yolks until creamy. Sift flour again with the baking powder and salt. Add dry ingredients alternately with milk to creamed mixture, mixing until smooth after each addition. Gently stir in drained blueberries. Beat egg whites until they form stiff peaks; fold them into other mixture. Turn batter into a greased 9-inch square pan, sprinkle brown sugar evenly over top, and bake in a moderately hot oven (375°, or 350° for glass pan) for 35 to 40 minutes. Cut into squares and serve warm. Makes 9 large servings.

BASIC MUFFINS

A perfect muffin depends on proper proportioning and technique. As in all formula-type recipes for baking, amounts of ingredients may vary. Our muffin recipe balances ingredients to create a slightly sweet muffin which displays all the desirable characteristics: tender but slightly coarse texture, pebbly browned surface, fairly even shape. Follow mixing directions carefully to avoid such classic pitfalls of muffin making as tunnels, toughness, and humps.

2 cups regular all-purpose flour
    (sift before measuring)
3 tablespoons sugar
1 tablespoon baking powder
½ teaspoon salt
1 egg
¼ cup melted butter or salad oil
1 cup milk

Sift flour again with sugar, baking powder, and salt into a bowl. Make a well in the center. Beat egg with butter and stir into milk. Pour all at once into flour well. Stir just to moisten ingredients, with about 12 to 15 full circular strokes that scrape the bottom of the bowl; batter will look lumpy. Grease muffin cups or line with baking cup liners; fill ⅔ full with batter. Bake in a hot oven (425°) for about 25 minutes or until well browned. Makes 10 muffins, ½ cup size.

Pebbly surface, feathery texture, and medium-coarse grain indicate a good muffin.

FIG AND ORANGE MUFFINS

Mix ½ cup chopped dried figs (Calimyrna or Mission) and ¾ teaspoon grated orange peel with dry ingredients in Basic Muffin recipe. Blend and bake as directed in basic recipe. Serve with orange marmalade.

Pour blended liquids into well made in dry ingredients.

Count strokes—12 to 15 full circular stirs will blend batter.

Spoon batter into greased muffin tin (or paper baking cup liners).

MACADAMIA MUFFINS

Follow recipe for Basic Muffins, adding ½ to ⅔ cup chopped macadamia nuts to dry ingredients. Mix and spoon into muffin cups as directed in basic recipe. Drop a spoonful of pineapple, papaya, or poha jam, or guava jelly into the center of each muffin (takes about ½ cup). Bake as directed for Basic Muffins.

TOASTED FILBERT MUFFINS

Add ½ cup very finely chopped toasted filberts to dry ingredients in Basic Muffin recipe. (To toast filberts, arrange nuts in a single layer in a shallow baking pan and place in a 350° oven for 15 to 20 minutes, shaking occasionally. Cool slightly; rub off as much of the brown husk as possible, then chop.) Mix and spoon into muffin cups as directed in Basic Muffin recipe. If you like, sprinkle batter with a mixture of 3 tablespoons of the finely chopped toasted filberts and 1 tablespoon sugar. Bake as directed for Basic Muffins.

WALNUT AND HONEY MUFFINS

Use ¼ cup honey instead of the sugar in Basic Muffin recipe, and decrease milk by 2 tablespoons. Blend honey with liquid ingredients. Add to dry ingredients ⅔ cup finely chopped walnuts, ½ teaspoon cinnamon, and ¼ teaspoon nutmeg; blend. Bake as directed in Basic Muffin recipe.

PEACH AND BROWN SUGAR MUFFINS

To dry ingredients in Basic Muffin recipe add ½ cup dried peaches, ¼ teaspoon soda and ⅛ teaspoon allspice; use ⅓ cup firmly packed brown sugar instead of the granulated sugar. Omit milk and blend 1 cup sour cream with liquid ingredients. Mix and bake as directed in basic recipe. If you like, sprinkle unbaked muffins with a little more brown sugar.

PEAR AND ANISE MUFFINS

Add to dry ingredients in Basic Muffin recipe ¾ cup chopped dried pears, ½ teaspoon anise seed, and ½ teaspoon grated lemon peel. Mix well and add liquids. Blend. Bake as directed in basic recipe.

DATE-PECAN MUFFINS

Serve these crunchy little muffins with a salad luncheon.

  2 eggs, well beaten
  1 cup raw sugar or brown sugar,
    firmly packed
  ½ teaspoon vanilla
  ⅔ cup regular all-purpose flour
    (sift before measuring)
  ¼ teaspoon baking powder
  ¼ teaspoon salt
  ¾ cup finely chopped dates
  ¾ cup finely chopped pecans or
    other nuts

Combine eggs with sugar and vanilla. Sift flour again with baking powder and salt into egg mixture. Add dates and nuts. Mix until well blended and spoon into buttered small muffin pans, filling them about ⅔ full. Bake in a hot oven (400°) for about 10 minutes or until lightly browned. Remove from pans and cool. Makes 16 small muffins.

LEMON MUFFINS

Fresh lemon juice and peel give these tender muffins pronounced tartness.

½ cup (¼ lb.) butter or margarine
¼ cup sugar
3 eggs
1 cup regular all-purpose flour
    (sift before measuring)
1 teaspoon baking powder
½ teaspoon salt
½ cup undiluted frozen lemonade
    concentrate, thawed

Cream butter and sugar together until fluffy; add eggs and beat until light. Sift flour again with baking powder and salt; add to the creamed mixture alternately with lemonade. Fill greased muffin cups ⅔ full with batter. Bake in a moderately hot oven (375°) for 20 minutes, or until delicately browned. Makes 15 two-inch muffins.

OATMEAL MUFFINS

Oatmeal gives these rather sweet muffins a distinctive texture. Either quick-cooking or regular oats may be used.

1 cup rolled oats
1 cup buttermilk
1 cup regular all-purpose flour
    (sift before measuring)
½ teaspoon salt
½ teaspoon soda
1½ teaspoons baking powder
½ cup melted shortening or salad oil
½ cup brown sugar, firmly packed
1 egg, beaten

Combine oats and buttermilk and soak for 30 minutes or longer. Sift flour again with salt, soda, and baking powder. Add melted shortening, brown sugar, and beaten egg to oatmeal mixture and blend thoroughly. Stir in dry ingredients and mix

only long enough to moisten. Spoon into greased muffin pans and bake in a moderate oven (350°) for 25 minutes or until brown. Makes 12 medium-sized muffins.

CORN-PINEAPPLE MUFFINS

Crushed pineapple in the batter and pineapple preserves baked on top make these tiny cake-like muffins especially flavorful.

1½ cups regular all-purpose flour
    (sift before measuring)
2 tablespoons sugar
4 teaspoons baking powder
1 teaspoon salt
1 cup yellow corn meal
2 eggs, beaten
1¼ cups milk
¼ cup (⅛ lb.) melted butter or
    margarine
½ can (8½ oz. size) crushed
    pineapple, drained
    Pineapple preserves

Sift flour again with sugar, baking powder, and salt. Stir in corn meal. Combine eggs with milk, melted butter, and crushed pineapple. Add to corn meal mixture, stirring just enough to moisten the dry ingredients. Spoon into greased small muffin tins, filling each tin about ⅔ full. Drop pineapple preserves from a ¼-teaspoon measuring spoon on top of each muffin. Allow to stand about 15 minutes. Bake in a hot oven (425°) for 20 minutes or until golden brown. Makes about 36 small muffins.

Inside crisp popover, the few thin, eggy walls make perfect retainers for pockets of jam, melted butter.

POPOVERS

Perfect popovers—tall, crisp, and almost hollow—are not at all difficult to make. The ingredients are few and basic; but measurements must be accurate to ensure success. You can bake popovers in almost any cup-shaped containers—lightweight, shiny metal muffin pans; dark, heavy cast-iron popover pans; ovenproof glass custard cups.

> 1 cup regular all-purpose flour
>   (sift before measuring)
> ¼ teaspoon salt
> 1 teaspoon sugar (optional)
> 1 tablespoon melted butter or
>   salad oil
> 1 cup milk
> 2 large eggs

In a bowl, mix flour with salt and sugar. Add butter or oil, milk, and eggs, and beat with a hand beater (or electric beater at medium-high speed) until very smooth, scraping bowl frequently with a rubber spatula; this takes about 2½ minutes. Fill greased baking cups about half full with the batter. Bake on center rack of oven until well browned and firm to touch—in a hot oven (400°) for about 40 minutes for a richly browned shell with a fairly moist interior, or in a moderately hot oven (375°) for 50 to 55 minutes for a lighter-colored popover, drier inside. (Keep oven door closed; popovers are extremely susceptible to collapsing if a draft of air hits them just as they are swelling above the cup, usually about ¾ of the way through the baking time.) Remove from pans and serve hot. Makes 12 popovers baked in ⅓-cup size pans, 10 popovers baked in ½-cup size pans; or 8 or 9 popovers baked in 5 or 6-ounce oven-proof glass cups.

If you like the interior of the popovers to be especially dry, loosen from pan but leave sitting at an angle in cups; prick popovers' sides with a skewer and let stand in the turned-off oven, door slightly ajar, for 8 to 10 minutes.

How popover forms: Thin batter has just been placed in hot oven.

About 10 minutes later: Batter starts to rise, form rigid walls.

After 20 minutes: Quaking motions occur as steam pushes walls.

After about 25 minutes: Popover slowly nears top of baking cup.

Popover literally pops out of cup a few minutes later.

At full size, beginning to brown, popover makes peak within cone.

WHIPPED CREAM BISCUITS

Whipped cream is both the shortening and moistening ingredient in these fluffy biscuits.

*1½ cups unsifted regular all-purpose
      flour
¾ teaspoon salt
4 teaspoons baking powder
1 cup heavy cream, whipped*

Measure flour, salt, and baking powder into a large bowl. Blend in the whipped cream with a fork until a stiff dough forms. Turn onto floured board and knead slightly. Roll dough out to about ½-inch thickness. Cut into rounds with a 2-inch cooky cutter. Place well apart on an ungreased baking sheet and bake in a hot oven (425°) for 10 to 12 minutes, or until golden brown. Serve immediately with butter and your favorite jam, jelly, or honey. Makes 16 2-inch biscuits.

BEATEN BISCUITS

Pale gold beaten biscuits make a crisp treat for breakfast, lunch, or tea. Beaten biscuits are especially good when reheated and served with lots of butter. You can split them apart so evenly that they seem to be made in layers.

  3 cups regular all-purpose flour
      (sift before measuring)
  1 teaspoon sugar
  ½ teaspoon salt
  ⅓ cup shortening (can be part butter)
  ½ cup milk

Sift flour again with sugar and salt. Cut in shortening very finely. Add milk to make a stiff dough. Put dough on a block and beat with a blunt wooden mallet until dough blisters; this takes about 20 to 25 minutes. Fold edges of dough in toward the center frequently. Roll dough about ⅜ inch thick and cut with very small biscuit cutter; prick biscuits with a fork. Bake in moderate oven (350°) for 30 minutes. Serve hot or cold. Makes 4 dozen 1½-inch biscuits.

BRAN SHORTCAKE BISCUITS

For a change from the usual shortcake base, try these biscuits made with bran and buttermilk. They're also good toasted for breakfast.

  ½ cup whole bran
  ¾ cup buttermilk
  1½ cups regular all-purpose flour
      (sift before measuring)
  1 teaspoon baking powder
  ½ teaspoon soda
  1 teaspoon salt
  2 tablespoons sugar
  ½ cup shortening
  1 tablespoon melted butter or
      margarine

Combine the bran with buttermilk, and let stand until most of the moisture has been taken up. Sift flour again with baking powder, soda, salt, and sugar into a bowl. Cut in the shortening until the mixture resembles cornmeal. Add the bran mixture and stir until blended. Turn out on a lightly floured board and knead lightly several times. Roll to a thickness of ½ inch; brush with the melted butter. Fold in half and again roll to ½ inch. Cut out with a floured cutter (about 2¾ inch size). Place on greased baking sheet and bake in a hot oven (400°) for about 15 minutes. Makes 8 biscuits.

DEVILED HAM AND CHEESE TWISTS

Serve these savory twists with a crisp green salad or a vegetable soup.

  2 cups prepared biscuit mix
  ½ cup shredded sharp Cheddar cheese
  ⅔ cup milk
  2 tablespoons melted butter
  1 large can (4½ oz.) deviled ham

In a bowl, combine biscuit mix with Cheddar cheese. Stir in milk. Turn dough onto floured board and knead lightly 4 or 5 times. Roll out to ¼-inch thickness, making a rectangle 12 by 24 inches. Brush with melted butter. Spread dough with deviled ham to within 1 inch of outside edges. Fold lengthwise (dough will measure 6 by 24 inches); pinch edges to seal. Cut into ½-inch strips (6 inches long) and twist each; place on greased baking sheet. Bake in moderately hot oven (375°) for 12 to 15 minutes. Serve hot. Makes 18 to 24.

Serve one or a selection of these breads to accompany soup or salad: (left to right), Cinnamon Sticks, Deviled Ham and Cheese Twists, Cheese Logs (page 94), Peanut Butter Corn Sticks.

PEANUT BUTTER CORN STICKS

These corn sticks are an excellent accompaniment for hot soups.

> 1 cup regular all-purpose flour
>   (sift before measuring)
> 3 teaspoons baking powder
> ½ teaspoon salt
> 1 tablespoon sugar
> ½ cup yellow corn meal
> ¼ cup plain or crunch-style
>   peanut butter
> 1 egg, slightly beaten
> ¾ cup milk

Sift flour again with baking powder, salt, and sugar into a bowl. Stir in corn meal. With a fork, cut in peanut butter until mixture resembles coarse crumbs. Combine egg with milk; stir in until dry ingredients are moistened. Grease corn stick pans well and fill two-thirds full. Bake in a hot oven (425°) for 12 to 15 minutes. Serve immediately. Makes 12 corn sticks.

CINNAMON STICKS

Almost like cookies, these are especially good with a fruit salad.

> 1 egg
> ½ cup sugar
> ½ teaspoon salt
>   Dash of cayenne
> ½ cup (¼ lb.) butter
> 2 cups regular all-purpose flour
>   (sift before measuring)
> 3 tablespoons sugar
> 1 teaspoon cinnamon

In a small bowl, beat together the egg, the ½ cup sugar, salt, and cayenne; set aside. Cream butter until soft. Add flour to butter alternately with egg mixture. Mix until dough is smooth. Combine the 3 tablespoons sugar and cinnamon. Shape dough into long strands, ½ inch thick, and cut into 4-inch pieces. Roll each in cinnamon sugar and place on a greased baking sheet. Bake in a moderate oven (350°) for 8 to 10 minutes, or until firm. Makes 36.

Shape dough for scones into two rounds; cut in quarters; separate wedges before baking.

Serve crisp-crusted scones fresh and hot, and with lots of butter and homemade jam.

OLD-FASHIONED CREAM SCONES

Scones are very close relatives of biscuits. In very old recipe books they called for no leavening at all and were always baked on a griddle, almost like a pancake. Some scones call for yeast, and some have no egg in them. Our version is rich, egg-flavored, and has a sugary top crust. It's baked in the oven.

    2 cups unsifted regular all-purpose
        flour
    3 teaspoons baking powder
    2 tablespoons sugar
    ½ teaspoon salt
    4 tablespoons butter or margarine
    2 eggs, beaten (reserve 1 tablespoon
        egg white for brushing on top)
    ⅓ cup heavy cream
    2 teaspoons sugar

In a bowl combine the flour, baking powder, the 2 tablespoons sugar, and salt. With a fork, cut in the butter until mixture resembles fine crumbs. Stir in the eggs and cream to make a stiff dough.

Turn out onto a lightly floured board and knead lightly until dough sticks together. Divide into two parts. Roll each part out to make a circle about 6 inches in diameter and about 1 inch thick. With a knife, cut each circle into quarters, making even wedges. Arrange on an ungreased baking sheet about 1-inch apart. Brush tops of scones with the reserved egg white and sprinkle with the 2 teaspoons sugar. Bake in a hot oven (400°) for 15 minutes or until golden brown. Serve immediately. Makes 8 scones.

CHEESE LOGS

These are rolled in sesame seed or poppy seed before they are baked.

    ½ cup (¼ lb.) soft butter
    2 teaspoons hot water
    1½ cups regular all-purpose flour
        (sift before measuring)
    ½ cup shredded sharp Cheddar cheese
    ¼ teaspoon curry powder (optional)
    1 egg, beaten
        Sesame seed or poppy seed

In small bowl of electric mixer, whip butter on medium speed for 2 minutes, adding hot water gradually. Add flour, mixing to make a soft dough. Stir in cheese and curry powder. Chill until stiff enough to handle. On floured board, roll dough into logs ½ inch in diameter; cut into 2-inch pieces. Brush with beaten egg, roll in sesame seed or poppy seed, and place 1 inch apart on greased baking sheet. Bake in a moderately hot oven (375°) for 12 minutes or until firm. Makes 48.

INDEX

Photographers: All photographs in this book are by Darrow M. Watt except as follows: Clyde Childress, page 57; Glenn M. Christiansen, pages 26, 41, 44 right, 54, 61 bottom, 84, 87, 93; Bruce Harlow, pages 52, 53; Blair Stapp, pages 25, 58. **Cover photograph:** Finnish Easter bread (page 54), by Darrow M. Watt. **Illustrated by** William Gibson, Jr.